D1605692

Virtual Afterlives

VIRTUAL AFTERLIVES

Grieving the Dead in the Twenty-First Century

CANDI K. CANN

UNIVERSITY PRESS OF KENTUCKY

Scholarly publisher for the Commonwealth,
serving Bellarmine University, Berea College, Centre College of
Kentucky, Eastern Kentucky University, The Filson Historical Society,
Georgetown College, Kentucky Historical Society, Kentucky State
University, Morehead State University, Murray State University,
Northern Kentucky University, Transylvania University, University of
Kentucky, University of Louisville, and Western Kentucky University.
All rights reserved.

Editorial and Sales Offices: The University Press of Kentucky
663 South Limestone Street, Lexington, Kentucky 40508-4008
www.kentuckypress.com

Library of Congress Cataloging-in-Publication Data

Cann, Candi K.
  Virtual afterlives : grieving the dead in the twenty-first century /
Candi K. Cann.
    pages cm
  Includes bibliographical references and index.
  ISBN 978-0-8131-4541-9 (hardcover : alk. paper) —
  ISBN 978-0-8131-4543-3 (pdf) — ISBN 978-0-8131-4542-6 (epub)
  1. Memorialization—Social aspects. 2. Death—Social aspects.
3. Bereavement—Social aspects. 4. Internet—Social aspects. I. Title.
  GT3390.C36 2014
  393—dc23   2014003472

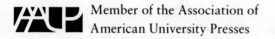

This book is dedicated to my brother
Kelly Ryan Cann (1972–2012).

Kelly, here are thousands and thousands of paragraphs
just for you!

I love and miss you.
Thanks for being my little brother.

Never again will the real have the chance to produce itself—such is the vital function of the model in a system of death, or rather of anticipated resurrection, that no longer gives the event of death a chance.

—Jean Baudrillard

I believe that ghosts are part of the future and that the modern technology of images . . . like cinematography and telecommunication . . . enhances the power of ghosts and their ability to haunt us.

— Jacques Derrida

Contents

Preface

I sent the initial project proposal for this book to the publisher the same day my brother collapsed and was taken to the hospital. He died less than forty-eight hours later, and I went to the funeral home to help make arrangements for his cremation on my way to the Columbia University Seminar on Death, where I presented the first draft of my chapter on Internet memorialization. Writing this book while mourning has made this manuscript deeply personal, relevant, and sometimes difficult, but it has been a gift, as I have been able to connect my research to my own bereavement journey.

The difficulty with death is that it is disruptive. It comes when we least expect it, even though we may have done everything we could to plan for it. We mourn the dead whose very absence is being disappeared. Contemporary society denies the place of the dead in both literal and figurative ways: corpses are relegated to burial in cemeteries outside the city center or are burned to ashes, whereas remembrance of the dead is often shortened or denied altogether. We speak of "moving on" and "moving forward"; we busy ourselves with plans to memorialize and make museums for remembrance. But the dead have gone missing from the realm of the living—they are, like their memorials, repackaged, the very disjuncture of death denied in its most crucial moment. This book first emerged from my doctoral work on martyrs and the way in which they are remembered and then repackaged in narrative stories. As I conducted that work, I also watched the developing popularity of grassroots memorialization and the ways in which people construct their own discourses of remembrance for the dead. These popular expressions of memorialization are not that different from martyr narratives, in that both seek to create meaning from death, while also seeking recognition for the bereaved. Grassroots memorialization is not limited to the American context, however, and this book is an examination of the phenomena of memorialization in the United States in a comparative perspective.

It is by no means exhaustive, but it does attempt to give a glimpse of which aspects of popular memorialization that are growing here are also surfacing in Asia and Latin America.

Ultimately, this book seeks to answer *why* this is occurring. I believe that memorialization has increased so much because death itself is disappearing. As in Baudrillard's quote, the dead are being resurrected—in religious afterlives or memorial ones, and death is being eclipsed by the act of remembering. What is also important, though, is the ways in which memorializing democratizes death and gives a voice to marginal grievers—those who are not given a place in society to grieve, either because of their position in society or because the type of death they have experienced is considered taboo or is not publicly sanctioned. Death is disruptive, but, ultimately, it is only because of death that we have life.

Introduction

American Grief: A Brief Historical Background

The face of grieving in American culture has changed dramatically in the last two hundred years. Traditionally, there were established grieving rituals that one followed after a death—mourning was a liminal state in which one withdrew from society and could grieve the dead, and then return to social norms and expectations. Evidence of such mourning rituals was fairly universal and included the wearing of mourning clothing and observing a certain period of enforced bereavement, during which one was both expected and permitted to take time off from traditional social events such as dinners, dances, and so on. One would also take time from one's occupational duties, after which one would generally reenter the world and participate in everyday social and work activities, commemorating the anniversary of the death on a regular basis. These traditional grieving rituals occurred during a time when people themselves were still in charge of most of the aspects of both dying and death, giving care to those dying in the home; washing, dressing, and preparing the body for the funeral following the death; and then disposing of the dead in the local cemetery or churchyard.

Over the last couple of hundred years, however, grief in the United States and the ways in which it is observed have drastically changed; several major events accompanied this transition of grief and mourning: the Industrial Revolution, the American Civil War, and advances in health care and medicine. The Industrial Revolution helped lead to the compartmentalization of work, so that it was no longer tenable to care for the dying and the dead. Workers labored long hours, and it wasn't practical to keep bodies in the home in large cities, where sanitary conditions were minimal and largely dependent on one's neighbors. Having dead bodies in such close quarters was not viewed as a practical or desirable situation and was socially

1

frowned on. The fragmentation or specialization of work occurred simultaneously with the development of death specialists, embalmers and funeral home directors, who contributed to the notion that bodies should be disposed of in a particular way. With the Industrial Revolution, it was not only jobs that became compartmentalized; death itself was removed from the realm of the living, as the management of death shifted away from the home to the funeral industry. Contributing to this trend were the medical and health industries, which moved dying from the home to the hospital. Ironically, medical advances accompanied the trend of shifting dying and death away from the realm of the living, and thus one could expect to end one's days in a hospital, where, upon death, the corpse would be transferred to the morgue and the funeral home.[1] Both dying and death were effectively taken out of church and home, leaving little or no contact between the living and the dead.

The American Civil War contributed to this trend with its large numbers of war dead, which created an impetus for finding a way to preserve bodies until they were delivered to the family of the deceased. Embalming thus became an expected and accepted part of the death practices in the United States. Though embalming has been practiced throughout history (in Egypt, for example, the mummification of important personages was common), it has not always been available to or expected for the masses, as it generally involved specialists and was not financially feasible for the average person. The democratization of death and the rise of the middle class allowed access to embalming practices that previously had been in the realm of only the few, and with the inventions of both refrigeration and the railroad—which resulted in refrigerated cars and the easy transport of corpses—the embalming of corpses for return to the families of the dead became an everyday reality. Embalming the body in the United States today is the norm rather than the exception.[2]

The Shroud and the Displacement of Death

Death and dying, with rare exceptions, have become compartmentalized from everyday life, and death and dying are a business. Along with the displacement of the care of dead bodies, the bereavement service itself, in the form of the funeral, has also moved out of the hands of the family and into the professional services of the funeral home. Funeral home directors often employ the title of "Bereavement Counselor" to describe one who is given the task of selling the family the various accouterments of death: the casket, embalming services, arrangement of the funeral or memorial service, and securing a resting place for the deceased. These "Bereavement Counselors" are indeed specialists in death, but they also walk a fine line between counseling families in their loss and selling packages that might maximize the funeral home's profit margins. This is a radical change from the death experience just a couple of hundred years ago, when caring for both the sick and dying and for the dead body itself was an expected part of one's everyday experience, and one constructed the casket oneself. Philippe Ariès traces this shift in attitudes about death in his book *The Hour of Our Death,* tracing the social construction of death from its previous place as a communal experience to the more individualized understanding of death as we see it today. According to Ariès, inscriptions on tombstones (which are becoming less popular as land becomes scarcer) and the proliferation of wills are indicative of the social importance of the individual and the decline of the community, influencing the ways in which we perceive and understand death.[3] Additionally, definitions of death itself have shifted since the 1950s and 1960s, and the emergence of new technology—defibrillators and respirators—has shifted the understanding of death from cardiopulmonary death to those of whole-brain and partial-brain death. Death, and its definition, is not only a social construction, but culturally determined, and the American understanding of death—like the corpse—is clean, sterile, sanitized, and based on a profound sense of the importance of the individual.[4] The image today for a dead body is not the corpse—but the shroud—the ugliness of death covered, and hidden away, if not cosmetically covered over.

Bereavement Leave: A Global Examination

Grief similarly has shifted from the everyday realm and no longer has a place in our society. In fact, grief has become marginalized by both society and the workplace, as bereavement policies are no longer the norm but the exception. Though the United States has a federal Family Medical Leave Act (FMLA), beyond this there is no official federal- or state-driven bereavement policy. Employers and society both expect the bereaved to return to work in a short time, and most American employees today are given only a maximum of three days off to make funeral arrangements and mourn. This decrease in bereavement leave has occurred in nearly direct correlation with the decline in traditional observances of mourning. To illustrate this point, a brief review of benefits and bereavement policies around the world reveals that among the most industrialized societies, the United States and the United Kingdom have no national bereavement laws; bereavement policies are enforced at the corporate or the local level. These leave policies generally allow anywhere from one to three days of paid leave;[5] further leave, if granted, is unpaid, though one can usually take sick leave or personal leave in addition to bereavement leave if one wishes to do so. Also, bereavement is generally defined for a very small group of mourners, identified as the "immediate family," consisting of parent, child and spouse. Grandparents, siblings, cousins, domestic partners, extended family, and friends are often not included in American and British policies on bereavement.[6]

In contrast, in Europe (particularly in those countries with more socially minded governments) workplaces generally offer a generous bereavement leave of anywhere from five days to four weeks, and many policies benefit and recognize same-sex marriages.[7] Bereavement policies in these countries are federally mandated and implemented at the company level. In Asia and Latin America one also finds federally mandated bereavement leave. In China national laws mandate a minimum of three to five paid days of bereavement leave, and additional leave is granted for travel if necessary, with the stipulation that the person must cover the cost of his or her own travel.[8] The Japanese government grants people ten days of paid bereavement leave for immediate family members and five days for extended family members, but most people take two or three times this amount to mourn and put family affairs in order.[9] In Chile federal bereavement leave grants seven days of paid leave for a spouse or a child, and three days for a parent, parent-in-law, or unborn child, and additional leave is granted if requested, but the minimum is guaranteed by the federal government.[10] In Colombia, federal law dictates that, no matter what type of employment, workers be given at least five paid days of leave for a spouse or "permanent companion" and any family member up to the second degree of blood kinship (in other words, parents, siblings, uncles, aunts, grandparents, and first cousins) and adopted members in the immediate family.[11] Thus, one views the differences in bereavement between the United States and other parts of the world: not only is bereavement not granted or protected by the American government, but the recipients of bereavement leave are often limited to immediate family and narrowly defined understandings of "family."

American Grief Revisited: Bereavement Policies Today

A brief examination of American bereavement policies in both the American government and private sector bears this out. Companies are not required to give bereavement leave and may demand that employees provide documentation of the death (a copy of either the death certificate or the obituary), or take any time off out of their personal and sick leave (or both). The usual amount of time granted, *if* it is granted, is three days, and this is extended only for immediate family: a parent, spouse, or a child. Grandparents, aunts, uncles, cousins, domestic partners, and so on, are not usually included in bereavement leave, although sometimes a workplace may grant time off for attending the funeral itself. The U.S. government generally grants its employees three days of bereavement leave for combat-related death for immediate family; employees are then able to use their personal and sick leave (up to thirteen days) for any additional days. If a family member dies from natural causes, employees use their sick days to cover their bereavement needs. Interestingly, the government's definition of family members is much wider than most policies in the private sector and includes the following: "spouse; parents; parents-in-law; children; brothers; sisters; grandparents; grandchildren; step parents; step children; foster parents; foster children; guardianship relationships; same sex and opposite sex domestic partners; and spouses or domestic partners of the aforementioned, as applicable."[12] In short, though little time is given to cover the needs for bereavement, the American government does grant bereavement leave to government employees for a wide definition of family, including domestic partners and extended family. Having no federal bereavement policy in the United States, and leaving it to individual companies to dictate, problematizes the notion of grieving, as there is no unified approach to bereavement, and companies can give priority to their profit margins over the well-being of their employees. It is no wonder, then, that in the United States grief has become so marginalized.

A brief survey of some companies across the United States reveals fairly standard bereavement leave policies. The general standard for full-time, non-exempt (salaried) employees is three days of bereavement leave. Hourly employees are often given only enough time off to attend the service or funeral, or they are simply told they must take unpaid time. The divide between the middle class and working poor becomes most evident in death—the working poor are given even less time to grieve than those who are salaried. While death comes equally to all, mourning does not. Most companies require documentation of not only the death, but also the relationship to the deceased, and, again, family is defined: bereavement policies dictate not only how long one mourns, but also *who* should be mourned. It would be impossible to give a list of all the various bereavement policies in the private sector, but I include here a few representative examples. Because companies are free to dictate their own bereavement policy, and there is no federally mandated law regarding bereavement, mourning is not protected, and employees are generally expected to negotiate their bereavement time on an individual basis with their employers. Additionally, many companies don't make their bereavement policies public knowledge, which makes access to and analysis of such policies difficult.

I illustrate the private sector's bereavement policy by giving two examples—one from Disney, considered to be a family-friendly company, and the other from AOL, chosen because it is one of the companies that has led the way in flextime and use of more family-friendly work schedules. I chose these companies because they are by far the most generous in their bereavement leave policies of companies in the private sector, yet even these companies do not come close to bereavement policies instituted in other countries with federally mandated guidelines in place. I will end with a brief comparison to Walmart—one of the largest employers in the United States, and a company with one of the poorest (yet more typical) bereavement policies in the private sector.

Disney, believed to be a generous company to work for, leads the way in private-sector policies regarding bereavement; it grants five days per event for regular employees for the following relationships between the deceased and the bereaved: "The deceased must be a spouse, qualified same-sex domestic partner, child, stepchild, grandchild, parent, parent-in-law, grandparent, or sibling of the employee. If an employee was especially close to or had responsibility for a relative other than these, bereavement leave may be granted by the head of Human Resources or a designated Human Resources representative."[13] Disney's leave policy of five days for regular employees is somewhat generous, and a broad range of relationships is addressed in its benefits handbook, including same-sex partners and siblings, and it allows for extra time given at the discretion of the Human Resources Department. According to Disney's employee handbook: "Payment is available only for scheduled work shifts which employees miss due to arrangement of, travel time to, and attendance at funeral services. Requests for bereavement leave must be made to and approved by the employee's immediate supervisor. The employee's relationship to the deceased and, upon request, the location and date of the funeral, must be provided in the request for bereavement leave."[14] This means that the time (up to five days in Disney's case) is applicable only for covering the actual time needed to make funeral arrangements, attend the funeral, and travel to and from the funeral. The "bereavement leave," like those of most companies in the United States, would be more aptly described as funeral attendance leave, as it covers only the shifts that interfere with the funeral. Additionally, employees are required, as they are in most companies, to provide documentation of the location of the funeral so that their supervisors may ascertain whether the bereavement leave request is reasonable. Disney provides its hourly employees bereavement leave at the rate of the scheduled shift, plus any additional pay that might have accrued. Disney's handbook states, "Payment for bereavement leave will be

made at the base wage or salary rate in effect at the time of the
leave. Shift premium and lead pay will be included in the computa-
tion of bereavement leave when applicable."[15] Thus, while employees are given time only to attend the funeral, rather than to
actually grieve, Disney is notable in its reimbursement to hourly
employees for shifts missed.

America Online's (AOL) bereavement policy is representative of
the standard corporate bereavement policy. Though its leave time for
salaried employees is more typical than Disney's, at three days rather
than five, AOL equals the playing field for salaried and hourly employees, giving them each three days off:

Bereavement Leave

AOL provides non-exempt (hourly) employees with up to 24 hours
of bereavement leave and exempt employees with up to 3 days
bereavement leave due to the death of an immediate family
member. Bereavement leave is granted at the Company's sole
discretion.

Eligibility for Bereavement Leave

The following employment classifications are eligible for
bereavement leave:

Full-time employee
Part-time employee

Procedure for Requesting Bereavement Leave:

Notify your manager as soon as possible of the need to take
bereavement leave. You may be required to provide appropriate
documentation as proof of your relationship to the deceased
person.

AOL recognizes the following as immediate family
members: Mother/Father Step-Mother/Step-Father Step-Sister/
Step-Brother Sister/Brother Spouse/Qualified Domestic
Partner Your Child, Step-Child, or Domestic Partner's
child. Grandchild Grandmother/Grandfather Mother-in-Law/
Father-in-Law Sister-in-Law/Brother-in-Law Anyone who acted in
a parental capacity or role when you were a child.

Bereavement Leave Policy

For non-exempt employees, you will be paid bereavement leave at 100% of your base rate of pay, based on the number of hours you are normally scheduled to work per week. For exempt employees, bereavement leave is paid at 100% of your base rate of pay at the time leave is taken. Paid bereavement leave is not considered in calculating overtime and does not include any special forms of compensation such as shift differential, incentives, commissions or bonuses. Non-exempt employees must report all bereavement leave taken on their timesheet for each payroll period. If you need additional time off after exhausting bereavement leave, you may request to take vacation or an unpaid personal leave of absence.[16]

AOL's bereavement leave is standard in the private sector and is actually far more generous in its definition of family than most companies: bereavement leave is granted here to those in mourning for their extended family and those who acted in a parental capacity, which includes such people as godparents and other unrelated significant persons. Grandparents and in-laws are also included here, which is highly unusual.

In contrast, Walmart's definition of family includes only the parents, children, and spouse, and paid bereavement leave is given only for these three categories of family. Anyone mourning someone outside this narrow definition of family (such as an uncle or a grandparent) may receive time off to attend the funeral, but the leave is unpaid. This can be an unnecessary hardship for hourly employees who depend on shift work for their pay. Additionally, to receive paid bereavement leave, employees must bring a copy of the death certificate or the obituary to their supervisor, proving that the death has occurred.[17] Like Disney and AOL, requiring the direct supervisor's approval for bereavement leave (as opposed to that of a human resources representative or, as in other countries, the federal government) often means that bereavement leave approval is subject to individual decision, rather than being a guaranteed right.

This brief study of various bereavement policies from the American government and the private sector is by no means comprehensive, but it does nonetheless reveal the range and variability of bereavement policies across the United States. The danger in this variability is that there are no shared societal expectations regarding bereavement. Bereavement leave would be more accurately titled Disposal Leave, as there is no time given to mourn and grieve the dead, only to dispose of them. Grief, then, is not only marginalized but highly individualized and dependent on many factors: one's status in society (whether one is a salaried or hourly employee), one's relationship with the bereaved, and one's relationship with one's supervisor all determine how one grieves, how long one is given to grieve (hours or days), and, ultimately, one's own individual resourcefulness for channeling that grief so that one can return to work as a productive employee. This is an enormous shift from just one hundred years ago, when grief was acceptable and a natural part of life, and death was seen as part of everyday experience.

Not having a federally mandated bereavement leave means not only that bereavement is not guaranteed or protected, but also that there is no socially accepted understanding of grief. Space, in the form of time, for grieving, is not given, and, as a result, grieving itself is highly marginalized, as workers are told how long and for whom they can and should grieve. Anyone grieving outside the mandated parameters has no time, space, or place in which to grieve. Even for officially sanctioned grief, however, three days is not enough time to dispose of the dead and mourn them. Three days is not enough time to meet with the coroners, plan a service, write an obituary, purchase the casket or the urn, embalm or cremate the body, buy a plot or a niche, hold the service, bury the dead, and then process and mourn the death. And this is even truer for those who do not meet the constraints of bereavement leave—domestic partners, for example—who are not granted any time from work to make all these final arrangements. Mourning is not only undesired in the workplace; it is undesired in American society. Death, a universal experience, and the mourning that helps us come to terms with our own fragility in life, has been pushed to the side in the social realm as well, as grief is now deemed a symptom of depression if it extends beyond two weeks.

American Grief or Mental Illness?

The American Psychiatric Association (APA) has pathologized grief so that it is no longer a meaningful or helpful part of everyday existence. In May 2013 the APA published its latest revision of its text, the fifth edition of the *Diagnostic and Statistical Manual of Mental Disorders* (*DSM 5*), which categorizes the various forms of mental illness.[18] This text is considered the gold standard of psychiatry and is, in part, used by insurance companies to determine what will and will not be covered under their insurance policies, and it is therefore updated every few years. One of the major changes between the *DSM* 4 and the *DSM* 5 was in the area of grief and bereavement. In the *DSM* 4 Major Depressive Disorder (MDD) could be diagnosed after two weeks of impaired functioning, but there was a bereavement exclusion, which essentially meant that those who were grieving the death or loss of a loved one were not considered to be clinically depressed because they were actually undergoing the bereavement process. According to the *DSM* 5, this exclusion no longer holds, and depression, even as a result or a part of grief, is considered to be an MDD if it extends beyond two weeks. While some herald this reclassification as a positive change because it allows for grief counseling to be reimbursed by insurance providers, classifying bereavement as depression after two weeks furthers the stigma of grief in our society and reveals how far we have moved from a time when grief and mourning were not only accepted but expected, and one who lost a family member could wear mourning clothing and abstain for a number of months, if not years, from daily social, occupational, and societal expectations.[19]

Additionally, this reclassification of grief removes the structural and social components of grief, through overfocusing on the individual and her or his experience of loss. When someone dies, not only is that individual gone, but the entire social fabric surrounding that individual has becomes disrupted, and social bonds change and shift in adjustment to the absence of the deceased. Categorizing grief as "normal," "abnormal," "extended," "prolonged," or simply stages to be worked through and beyond does not recognize the complexity of the disruption of death, nor does it take into account the immediate and traumatic social disruption that occurs when an individual dies. One does not simply lose the deceased, one also must relearn how to navigate and reinterpret one's social moorings and relationships without the dead. It is not only the person who dies, but the memories and the complex social relationships moored in that person that one loses through death.[20] In contemporary American society, this can be complex. With blended families, the loss of the primary biological parent does not merely serve to disrupt relationships, but, in extreme situations, can cause the severance of relationships and the loss of "home." To speak of grief in such simplistic terms as "stages to be moved through" does not do justice to the dramatic shifts that sometimes occur in the landscape of loss, nor does it take into account the complex social web of relationships that are affected by that loss. Glenys Caswell writes, "Although we might consider our memories to be private, there is an element of memory that is social and shared. . . . Some of a person's earliest and most intense memories come from the shared experiences of being in a family, and it is a well known phenomenon that memory can appear to change over time, and these are both aspects of memory that may be of significance in the funeral context."[21] Focusing on the individual experience of grief as stages to be moved through and beyond, as opposed to unpacking the social morass of bereavement, marginalizes grief further and prevents a true *communitas* of shared mourning.

Popular Memorialization: Grassroots Expression of Grief

Without the public acknowledgment or acceptance of mourning, grief is being pushed into the private realm, and as a result, new grieving traditions are emerging at the grassroots-popular-private level that are then introduced into the public sphere. Examples of some of these emerging bereavement traditions are bodiless memorials, tattoo memorials, car-decal memorials, T-shirt memorials, and Internet and social network memorials. People need not only to grieve, but also to be publicly recognized as bereaved, and these practices allow them to do that. As martyrs and martyr narratives have brought meaning to the deaths of those who have died and to those who are left behind, the bereavement practices emerging in the popular sphere reveal new ways of bringing meaning to the understanding of death. And just as martyr narratives often tell as much about the people championing a particular martyr, bereavement practices are often just as much about the grievers (if not more) than about the deceased themselves. Bereavement practices reveal an organic expression of the desire to be publicly identified as a griever. The liminal period of grief should be seen as part of the process of living. In the United States it is the denial of death and the refusal to allow grief in our daily lives that has contributed to the pathologization of grief. To examine this trend, it is important to examine the United States in a comparative lens, questioning whether this trend is a global one or whether it is unique to America.

In this book I will examine various forms of emerging popular memorialization, from the spontaneous memorials at the sites of the recent shootings in Aurora, Colorado, Nickel Mines, Pennsylvania, and Newtown, Connecticut, to the more personal expressions of mourning found in tattoos, car-decal memorials, T-shirts, and on the Internet. Situating this study as a comparative exercise allows us to see the particular influences on popular bereavement, and, I believe, also provides a notion of *why* and *how* these particular forms of bereavement are emerging. *All forms of alternative memorialization are emerging because of, and concurrent with, the disenfranchisement of mourning.* Bereavement is no longer given public space in society or culture, which forces people to create and adopt alternative forms of mourning to help them navigate public space with their altered status as grieving individuals. These alternatives are all popular forms of new grieving rituals, which allow the bereaved to grieve while remaining functional in a world without mourning. J. R. Averill and E. P. Nunley assert in their *Handbook of Bereavement* that "because of their importance, mourning practices are not simply quaint customs that can be ignored at will. On the contrary, they are duties imposed by the group," usually within established political and religious systems, which are those parts of society responsible for "collective decision making" and "meaning and value articulation."[22] Because of the marginalization of the discourse of grieving, and the disappearance of death,[23] mourners are forced to create new and original forms of mourning rituals, and, in turn, some of these, such

as Internet memorials, are developing their own rituals, which are replacing old religious rituals in providing meaning and explaining
death. Jennifer Clark and Majella Franzmann write, in agreement
with C. A. Haney, C. Leimer, and J. Lowery,[24] that "the presence of
spontaneous memorials, of which roadside memorials form a subset,
indicated a desire to reconstruct new forms of ritualized mourning
because traditional mourning practices were old fashioned, inade-
quate and perhaps even irrelevant to modern Americans."[25] Private
memorialization is thus now entering the public sphere and re-creat-
ing bereavement rituals that were previously socially sanctioned and
universally recognized. Spontaneous memorials are in some ways a
spectacle of grief, in the same way that violence and sex have become
commodified and made spectacle. Grief must be acknowledged, and
the emergence of popular memorialization is evidence of that.

A *Chapter Outline of* Virtual Afterlives

In this book I examine four primary categories of popular memorialization, in an order that reflects the gradually disappearing body,
from material memorials at the site of a death to the Internet or social
network memorial, in which the body has completely disappeared
and is replaced by only a virtual remembrance. These four categories
are (1) Bodiless memorials (2) Tattoo memorials, (3) Car-decal and
T-shirt memorials, and (4) Internet and social network memorials.
The subject of the first chapter is bodiless memorials, which usually
memorialize the site of death, rather than the body, and reflect current society's denial of the corpse, displacing the dead body and temporarily transforming public space into a bereavement space. These
spaces, however, are becoming smaller in both geography and time,
as public memorialization either must be appropriated by the public
arena or forced back into the private realm. For example, the spontaneous memorial that emerged at the site of the shootings in Aurora,
Colorado, was allowed to remain for two months, and then the city
government removed it and is keeping the many items in the city ar-
chives for a future public memorial. Popular memorialization in
Newtown, Connecticut, however, was removed after two weeks, as
officials felt that two weeks was enough time to grieve, and "return

to normal." Public space for grieving is appropriated at the popular level, but the function of public space is in contention between those who are grieving and those who want to "return to normal." Additionally, time itself is appropriated and shifted according to competing notions of grief and what is "appropriate" and "inappropriate" grief. I argue in this chapter that it is, in part, the disappearance of the corpse that has led to these appropriations of both space and time. As Maurice Merleau-Ponty writes, "I am not in space and time, nor do I conceive space and time; I belong to them, my body combines with them and includes them."[26] The disappearance of the body precludes the shift in space and time. If the body is not present, then where are we to conduct our grief work, except in space and time?

Chapter 2 investigates tattoo memorials, in which a deceased person is remembered by being etched into the skin of the bereaved. They are another form of mourning clothing, but tattoos are permanent ways of marking grief and, in both virtual and literal ways, are forms of carrying the dead with us in a world where death and the corpse are denied. The body, though it has disappeared, is remapped onto living flesh to become a symbol of mourning in a world where mourning is denied. I also highlight the role of tattoo artists themselves in conducting grief work through the tattooing of the body, and I discuss the popularity of the body as a canvas for not only marginalized grieving, but also marginalized death. One finds tattoos mostly in honor of those whose deaths are not typically socially recognized in current parameters of grieving: friends, colleagues, infants, or grandparents. Deaths that one cannot publically acknowledge or discuss are generally found inscribed on bodies as personal tributes or memorials.

Car-decal and T-shirt memorials, in which a memorial of the deceased is placed on the windshield of a car or worn on a T-shirt and serves temporarily as a memorialization of the deceased, are the subject of chapter 3. Like tattoos—but less permanent—car decals and T-shirts allow grievers to claim status as bereaved so that grief work may be done in a socially accepted way. Car-decal and T-shirt memorials also allow the bereaved to make public their status as grievers, and yet, after a time, because of the memorials' temporary nature, mourners can return to their nongrieving states. These decals and T-shirts, like tattoos, are generally found among marginalized communities and are used by marginalized grievers—grievers who cannot express their grief in other socially acceptable ways, either because they are not "allowed" to grieve or because they are grieving for the socially unacceptable dead (usually babies or young adults). Almost all these memorials seem to have a virtual counterpart, and when popular and public grieving is "over" (as in Newtown), grieving is heavily present and prevalent in the virtual realm.

Internet memorials, including tombstone Internet links with virtual memorials, funeral home memorials, grieving websites, and spontaneous social network sites of a deceased person, the subject of chapter 4, illustrate that the language of grief is both popular and spontaneous. Internet grieving allows for marginal discourse to circumvent traditional modes of bereavement by reclaiming mourning discourse and the ways we talk about and think about the dead. This book moves from the displacement of the body in bodiless memorials to the most disembodied state—the virtual memorial—revealing the shift away not just from death, but from the dead body itself. It is the most disembodied form of remembering, but as we have made death, the dead body, and the grieving experience disappear from the public sphere, the virtual realm ironically returns with the specter of death to haunt us. The rise of shows such as *The Walking Dead, Twilight, Six Feet Under* all return the dead to us through the spectacle of death, and the virtual realm returns us to our mourning through memorialization—the dead body—presented through image and memory, without the messiness of the corpse. It is nearly the opposite of what occurs in the religious realm with martyrs and saints and the cult of relics. Martyrs and saints bring us closer to holiness and to God *through* their bodies, and the narratives of their suffering; but these memorials are ultimately popular attempts to bring back the dead, marginalized as they are by our culture and our own history in the understanding and treatment of the dead. Memorials function as replacements for the body, since we cannot keep the body among us; they must be reinscribed in public space, in material remembrance, etched into our bodies, pasted on our cars, worn on our bodies, or transfigured on our social-network sites. The dead will return to haunt us if we do not acknowledge them.

1

The Bodiless Memorial

The Dis-location of the Body

Grieving without Bodies

Recent years have seen an upsurge in spontaneous and grassroots memorialization[1] and the rise of popular memorials for the dead: the Columbine shooting memorial, the memorial of Diana outside Kensington Palace, the Oklahoma bombing memorial, the Aurora, Colorado, shootout memorial, the World Trade Center memorial,[2] and most recently the Sandy Hook Elementary School memorial. In addition to these large specters of public memorialization, there has been an enormous upswing in local and personal memorialization. Erika Doss discusses this trend in her recent book, *Memorial Mania*, documenting the phenomenon of memorialization in popular culture and its growing popularity.[3] The most curious aspect of this trend is the movement toward memorialization without the body. From spontaneous memorials to memorial services (as opposed to funerals), there is a key element missing: the dead body. Whether it is a memorial located at the place the body was last intact before its death, such as roadside memorials and the Sandy Hook Elementary memorial, or it is a memorial service held with cremated remains and no corpse, bodiless memorials are clearly indicative of the trend toward memorialization without bodies. In this chapter I address the displacement of the body in contemporary memorialization and question the possible problems and meanings behind this displacement. Then I analyze several of the more recent popular bodiless memorials that have emerged in the last ten years, including ghostbike memorials and memorials at the sites of the Nickel Mines tragedy, the Aurora, Colorado, movie theater shootout, and the Sandy Hook Elementary School killings.

The traditional purpose of the funeral is manyfold, but it has two primary functions: the ritual that allows the proper disposal of the body in a way that prepares the dead for the next phase of life after death, and the ritual working through of grief for the community that knew the dead person. Even those who do not believe in an afterlife, however, can acknowledge the funeral's purpose of providing for the "correct" disposal of the dead. (Whether religious or merely sanitary, the disposal of the corpse is still a necessary aspect of the funeral.) Prevalent in the last 150 years, however, has been the (primarily Western) cultural view of the necessity of the viewing of the embalmed corpse as a part of the remaining community's "grief work" over the dead person.[4] Death rituals traditionally emphasize the dead body as central to the ritual itself, providing an encounter with the dead that allows the bereaved to personally confront death. What then do we do without a body? What does it mean when we memorialize at the site of death as opposed to the location of the dead body itself? Bodiless memorials offer a way to express one's grief in a publicly sanctioned way, but without the confrontation of death and the corpse. Bodiless memorials—whether they are a spontaneous memorial at the site of death, or a service without the corpse—are a remembering and celebration of the body *without* the body. In short, a bodiless memorial is a disembodied memorial for the body. As Karen Wilson Baptist wrote about a personal memorial she attended in honor of a deceased colleague: "I sensed no comfort in this contemporary celebration of death. There was no casket, no urn, no body in the room. Nobody led us into ritual commemoration; rather there was an open microphone at the front of the room. Speak at will. Share a story. But we did not share stories nor did we sing laments together: there was no grave to attend to, no ashes to scatter."[5] Baptist goes on to write in this very personal encounter of how this bodiless memorial left her feeling emotionally disembodied—as though the deceased person being memorialized was somehow expected to be present yet gone—and how difficult this was for her own grief work. In short, the memorial allowed her to remember but not to encounter death itself. There is no space for grieving because without the encounter of the corpse itself, there is a fundamental denial of death, underscored by the missing body. The dead body has both figuratively and literally gone missing from death; but with this dis-placement of the body, death itself has become denied, and grieving itself becomes marginalized.

Bodies and their roles in death and bereavement can be highlighted by embalming—the desire to preserve them—and the emphasis placed on viewing them, or having them present. In this way, corpses become central actors in funerals and grieving ceremonies. The dead body, in its encounter by the grieving, actively helps in the bereavement process by impressing on the living that it is no longer present, but dead. But embalming also unnaturally preserves the body, and it is an attempt to preserve and present the body in such a way that it seems most like the living. Embalmment in the last century was not for the preservation of the body and its ultimate resurrection (as in ancient Egyptian society), but rather for the avoidance of the natural process of decay after death. In this way, embalmment was not, as it might first seem, a way of bringing us *closer* to the dead, but actually a way of further estranging us from them. The dead, as they are, are not presentable and acceptable company; they must first be sewn shut, stuffed, drained, transfused, and made up before we deem them acceptable. Dead bodies thus are no longer part of our lives unless they seem like the living.

Cremation, on the other extreme, completely obliterates the body so that it is no longer present. Cremation is on the rise in American funerary practices, while embalmment is still customary for the majority of deaths; but both are essentially ways of denying the body and the natural decomposition of the corpse. Embalmment, though it preserves the body so that it can participate in the funeral, does so in such a way that the horrors of death's decay are in many ways ignored and disregarded; cremation, on the other hand, destroys the body altogether. Clark and Franzmann write, "The recent and current popularity of cremation in the West may increase the tendency to divorce death from place even further by completely disposing of the mortal remains and reducing the likelihood of a continued physical connection between the mourners and the deceased."[6] Embalmment and cremation are two opposite indicators of a similar phenomenon in which the natural body in the form of the corpse is denied.

Another element of this denial of bodily death and decay can be seen in coffin purchases in American funeral homes. Some funeral directors have noted that the most popular coffin purchases are those that promise protection from external deterioration; the irony, of course, is that bodily decomposition occurs from within. It is the body itself that causes the deterioration of the body—not the influence of outside elements introduced into the coffin. Nevertheless, the most expensive options offer special elements such as "hermetically sealed coffins" and coffins made of metal alloys that are least likely to deteriorate from natural elements. These "extras" are useless, however, in protecting the corpse from deterioration. (These expensive coffins can, though, confer status on both the dead and the grieving family within their community and so are not entirely without utility.) Embalmment, cremation, and the purchase of special coffins to prevent decomposition are all indicative of a greater cultural phenomenon: the denial of death through a denial of the corpse. The dead body should remain out of sight, or if it is to participate in the funeral, it should do so disguised as a living body, in a close approximation of the person he or she was when living.

The Hidden Body and the Agency of the Corpse

Corpses are powerful in their own way: they help create cemeteries and columbaria, shaping the deathscape and affecting the ways in which the dead intersect with the world of the living.[7] Avril Maddrell and James Sidaway discuss the importance of funerals, cemeteries, columbaria, and the ways in which corpses help deathscapes become embedded with meaning.[8] Corpses have long held meaning for the living, even conferring sacredness onto a world previously mapped as ordinary. Martyr and saint relics, for example, help bestow sanctification onto a place, mapping the power of the corpse onto a geographical location so that it is no longer ordinary but sacred. From the relics of saints and martyrs in European churches to those of the Buddha and the Buddhist saints in Asia, corpses (and pieces of corpses, whether finger bones, teeth, or drops of blood) as agents of power and sanctification demonstrate that corpses have not only agency over the physical landscapes of the living, but religious agency as well.

The political agency of corpses can be seen in the veneration of the bodies of the dead (such as Mao in modern China[9] and Evita in Argentina[10] and, most recently, in the burial at sea of the body of Osama bin Laden[11]). Dead bodies are not passive recipients of action but, in fact, have their own agency and are capable of having, giving, and transferring agency.[12] Bodies in wars, suicide bombings, the World Trade Center attacks, or even the Sandy Hook Elementary shootings all take on a greater, more complex, and heavily imbued political meaning. Holocaust victims' bodies become powerful reminders of the cruelty of extreme nationalism, and corpses of suicide bombings tell tales of extreme belief and desperation and individual agency in the face of bureaucratic systems that sometimes carry religious power and transfer righteousness to its venerators. World Trade Center corpses carry with them the weight of disbelief and a justification for a new style of warfare that no longer follows traditional rules of conflict. The Sandy Hook Elementary shooting victims' bodies are inscribed with meaning, as they become powerful pawns in the battle over gun control and a questioning of the U.S. Constitution's Second Amendment. Bodies in the form of corpses are important because they are powerful and can be inscribed, reinscribed, covered, hidden, destroyed, exhumed, and metaphorically resurrected in the world of the living. Corpses, however uncomfortable they may make us, are essential to our grief: as R. P. Harrison writes, "For what is a corpse if not the connatural image, or afterimage of the person who has vanished, leaving behind a lifeless likeness of him- or herself. If the corpse embodies or holds on to the person's image at the moment of demise, funeral rites serve to disentangle that nexus and separate them into discrete entities with independent fates—the corpse consigned to earth or air, and the image assigned to the afterlife, whatever form that imaginary afterlife may take in this or that cultural framework."[13] The dead body, then, is not, as many have treated it, a passive and neutral actor in the funeral; rather, it is precisely because of the fear of its agency that dead bodies have recently been banished to reside in cemeteries on the city's outskirts, or laid to rest and trans-

22 VIRTUAL AFTERLIVES

formed into "natural" landscapes. The corpse is being disappeared from the realm of the living precisely because of its power and ability to make us uncomfortable.

What, then, does this mean for bodiless memorials? As Craig Young and Duncan Light write, "Dead bodies become material signifiers of power and agency. Why (or what meaning) then the need for bodiless memorials, where the body is secondary to the world of the living and its need for memorialization?"[14] The living need the presence of the dead body to help them digest the absence of the dead, and yet memorialization seems to be favoring the act of remembering. The disappearance (or banishment) of dead bodies from the world of memorialization is as intentional as it is disturbing. As Baptist writes, "Suspended within the living flesh, the dead exhibit a material subjectivity that simultaneously exhibits both presence and absence, mass, and void. Grief could be said to be haunted by this paradoxically dichotomous subjectivity that is marked by the desire to maintain a continuing bond between the isolated state of the bereaved and the corporeally tangible dead that requires displacement in order to activate 'recovery.'"[15] Thus, the disappeared body returns; it returns to haunt, in its absence, its rightful place in the circle of death and dying, and it does this through memorialization. The body, even dead, demands recognition. Bodiless memorials, whether found on the roadside, in a ghostbike, or outside a movie theater, are the body's way of remapping itself in the popular imagination, in much the same way that embalming erases signs of death and decay and returns the body, if only briefly, to the world of the living. What then, does this say about the *place* of memorials? What is the role of place in memorialization, if the body is not the focus?

Dis-locating Death: Sacred Space and Bodiless Place

Though dead bodies, or pieces of them, help sanctify a space, this act of sanctification is now no longer exclusively the realm of corpses, but also dependent on the memory of the living. The *place* of memorialization is important because of the memories of the living and the meaning assigned to the location in the context of grief and loss. Clark and Franzmann write, "The actual spot becomes sacred and is imbued with ritualized meaning by the creation of a memorial marker as a focus for grief and communication. Memorial makers feel authorized to claim that place for the deceased regardless of the designated purpose of that space."[16] In other words, it is not the dead body but, rather, the grief of the survivors that makes the place important. The need to memorialize, separate from the corpse, may be part of the impetus behind the proliferation of grassroots memorialization. In a world where the dead and their bodies are literally hidden, disappeared, or spirited away, memorialization offers a way in which survivors can reinscribe the dead into the realm of the living in a virtual and spatial way.[17] Memorials, whether they are tattoos, social network sites, car decals, T-shirts, or roadside memorials, all take geographical (material or virtual) space and, in this way, offer a substitute—albeit cleaner, neater, more sanitary, and less scary—for the physical remnants of the corpse. Additionally, grieving individuals determine the location of these memorial spaces, unlike deathscapes; the grieving experience is no longer relegated to the outskirts of the city, the borderlands of the living, but reinserted into the quotidian lives of the living. Memorials are mapped onto the geographical contexts of the living, forcing the realm of death back into the realm of the living, in ways that are not always publicly sanctioned. Additionally, Baptist and Grey Gundaker claim that material objects often left at these bodiless memorials (usually personal artifacts or items of clothing that once belonged to the deceased) can operate as material substitutions for the deceased, standing in as socially acceptable forms of the corpse.[18] As Baptist writes, "The pain of grief is evoked by corporeal withdrawal from the loved one. The material substitution for absence (the photograph, a familiar shirt, the roadside shrine in the landscape) creates a tangible presence for the dead, triggering pain but allowing the bereaved to direct their pain to something outside of the body. The pain of grief remains in the body until dispersed (although remnants always remain)."[19] Not everyone welcomes this intrusion of the dead into the realm of the living, however, and some have protested memorials and their assumptive claims to secular space.[20]

The Body and Its Place in Asia

In both Japan and China the notion of place is integral to the understanding of death and the afterlife. In Japan, when one is born, one's
birth is typically registered with the local Shinto shrine; upon death,
the deceased become *kami* (or spirits) who watch over the living. Additionally, following a death, for both Japanese Buddhists and Shinto
practitioners (nearly all Japanese observe Buddhist funerary customs
whether or not they consider themselves to be active Buddhists, and
Shinto customs are saved for the more "happy and auspicious" times of
one's life), a personal shrine is typically placed in the home, consisting
of a picture of the deceased, her or his name, a few personal objects,
and daily food and drink offerings, in addition to the daily recitation
of prayers, chanting, and the lighting of incense and candles. And
though cremation is generally customary, the corpse is usually washed,
dressed, and prepared in the home for cremation or burial; the undertaker comes to the family home to prepare the body, and family members help in these preparations. The care of the corpse is not outsourced,
but rather considered part of the ceremony for the disposal of the dead.
Afterward, burial or interment of the ashes is most often held in the
local Buddhist temple, generally located in the neighborhood itself,
within walking distance and easily and frequently visited. Following
the ceremony, the deceased's shrine inhabits the home, and though the
grave is maintained, the shrine serves as a functional replacement for
the corpse. At first, daily offerings and prayers are made at the shrine,
but after a year, the shrine can be moved to a more discreet place in the
home. This practice thus allows the ancestor to continue in some way
as part of the family, present for everything that occurs in the home,
but it also marks the presence of the deceased person's absence. It is not
surprising, then, that the trend of memorialization so popular in the
West is not really found in Japan. The few public tragedies in contemporary Japan (the subway gassings, for example, by Aum Shinrikyo)
did not inspire mass memorial responses.[21] Additionally, though most
may be buried on Buddhist temple grounds, many Japanese also visit
Shinto shrines, which allow for the conversion of dead ancestors into
kami, and this continued presence of the dead in people's lives permits
a way for the dead to retain a continued presence and relationship with

the living. The dead do not leave the realm of the living—rather, they merely change the way they interact with it.

In China, because of a land shortage, the state has led the initiative for cremation, which is almost universally followed. The exception, of course, is those who are powerful and wealthy enough to pay the requisite bribes to bring the corpse back to the ancestral home for burial, or those who live in the countryside, where some still manage to escape state regulations on disposal and burial. In Taiwan, however, the more traditional Chinese customs of body burial is still favored. In both countries funerals mark the transition of the living into the realm of the dead, and elaborate processions and funerals are held to honor the deceased. Though it is difficult to speak of "Chinese" funerary customs, as customs vary by locale and the government in mainland China has driven many of the state-sponsored initiatives regarding death and disposal, the Chinese worldview regarding death has been surprisingly resilient, even in Chinese American communities in the United States.[22]

Like those in Japan, the Chinese funeral marks a transition of the ways in which the living interact with the dead, rather than a complete break of the dead from the world of the living. In mainland China, until 1949, Chinese law dictated mourning customs, whereas today these are governed more by social pressure and societal dicta. Chinese law decrees that people be given a minimum of three days of paid bereavement leave. Previously, mourning periods ranged from three to twenty-seven months, and failure to observe proper codes of mourning was punishable by fines, beatings, imprisonment, or even exile from the community. In the Chinese Republican period these laws were abolished under Sun Yat-sen, who implemented a shorter mourning period, and then were further modified under the Communist regime, though funeral customs are still rather expressive and expensive. Generally, a wake is held in the home (though this is much more common in the countryside) or in the funeral home, and friends and family come to pay their respect for the dead. When the wake is held in the home, the corpse is prepared and placed in a particular room in the home, called a *ling tang* (spirit room), along with flowers, candles, offerings, food, and a picture of the deceased, for about seven days. The corpse is not left alone during the wake, and usually family members sit with the corpse for the duration of the week, both day and night. And though the Communist regime eliminated many popular religious beliefs, it is still common to consult a geomancer for the most propitious day on which to hold the funeral, to hire a Daoist specialist in feng shui for the disposal of the body, and to pay for a band to accompany the funeral procession, the loud noise of the band serving to scare away any lingering spirits. Generally, paper houses, paper cars, fake money, paper clothing, and cardboard cell phones and computers (now iPads and iPhones are all the rage in funeral paraphernalia) are offered to the deceased, while mourners attending the funeral give donations of flowers and money to the family to help cover the costs of the funeral. At the funeral, red (the color of happiness and of weddings) is generally avoided, and mourners are encouraged to wear white, considered the color for the dead, though now any somber and muted colors are considered acceptable. One of the gifts given to the families of the deceased is mourning cloth—cloth in colors used for both mourning clothing and to make armbands. Giving both cloth and money to the bereaved families helps subsidize costs traditionally associated with the funeral, and flower arrangements reveal the status of the dead (and his or her family) within society. Following the funeral, both men and women wear armbands denoting their mourning status to those around them. These armbands are worn from forty-nine to one hundred days over everyday clothing, though they can be worn for a lesser or greater amount of time, depending on the individual and his or her circumstances.

Death and grief in China continue to be a part of the social fabric of everyday life, though, as is true in the rest of the world, the length of time for bereavement has been shortened. The continued practice of wearing mourning clothing, along with the installment of the deceased person's family tablet (described in more detail below) in the home and the daily offerings made in honor of the deceased, however, allow for death to be a part of everyday life. The bereaved wear their status as mourners for a protracted length of time, and the living continue to interact with the dead and act out mourning rituals on a daily basis in a way that allows the dead to be present in the home and society. Having accepted and socially sanctioned grieving rituals allows mourning to be seen as a normative experience of daily life. When one dies in China, following the funeral, one's spirit is placed in a wooden tablet, by the writing of one's name in red ink, which is situated in the ancestral hall in one's home. (This can be as simple as putting the tablet in a specially designated corner of a home with other such tablets, or as elaborate as designating a specific room in the house or even a separate hall for such tablets.) The spirit of the deceased maintains its place with the living, and family members make regular offerings of food and other material objects (usually items the deceased enjoyed in his life, such as cigarettes, bottles of wine, favorite snacks, or even cardboard replicas of iPhones or iPads), maintaining a relationship of reciprocity between the living and the dead. The living make offerings to the deceased, giving items the dead can use in their afterlives, while the living receive the blessings and protection of the dead watching over them in return. Thus, while mainland China requires that its deceased be cremated, the bereaved still regularly interact with the living, and the *presence* of the dead in the realm of the living is maintained. In both Japan and China the *place* of memorialization is separated from the corpse; however, the dead inhabit the world of the living and retain strong emotional and material ties with the living.[23]

In the United States and Europe the dead are *displaced*. They are banished and no longer inhabit the world of the living. The recent upsurge in popular memorialization, whether on one's car, on one's skin, or alongside the road, is a way in which the dead body can be memorialized by substituting material objects that symbolize the dead for the body. Internet memorials are not material, but they are no less important in remapping the dead into the world. In a world in which the virtual intersects with the material in hundreds of ways (smart phones, the Internet, gaming, and so on), Internet memorials offer an alternative way in which corpses reinscribe their place in the world in palatable and presentable ways.

Cuerpos and Corpses: Death and the Body in Latin America

The most famous examples of memorialization in Latin America are dedicated to those who lost their lives during the political upheavals and military dictatorships from the 1960s to the late 1980s, but corpses retain their powerful political presence today through popular protest and terrorist resistance that use dead bodies as evidence of both political repression and political resistance. More famous examples include Che Guevara and Evita Perón. Following his execution in Bolivia, footage of Che Guevara was widely viewed as proof of the military regime's vanquishing of the revolutionary guerilla forces. Following her death, Evita's corpse was kidnapped and stuffed into a van on a side street for safekeeping, as her cadaver was controversial, a symbol of the Peronista regime, at once both revered and hated. Her body resurfaced years later, to be properly embalmed and buried, heralding the return of Juan Perón himself. From the disappeared in Argentina[24] to the assassination of Oscar Romero in El Salvador,[25] to the more recent drug cartel executions on a northern highway in Mexico,[26] corpses are evidence of the powerful political agency that they retain in the Latin American imagination.

In the religious realm, a close association of the Catholic dead with martyrs and saints inspires a complex ritual invoking the dead, exemplified by Mexico's celebration of the Day of the Dead.[27] Unique to Mexico, this holiday is similar to the practices found in China and Japan, in that an altar, on which are placed a picture of the deceased, material objects that the dead person favored, candles, incense, food, drink, and, finally, representations of the dead in the form of skeletons and skulls, constructed from papier-mâché or sugar, is erected in the home. The altar is placed on a mantel or in a prominent corner of the house, and it is essentially an invitation to departed spirits to rejoin the family in their home. What is important about this custom is that, as in the practices in Asia, the dead are reinvited into the realm of the living in a communal and socially accepted way. Thus, the dead inhabit the world of the living, and the living maintain their ties with the dead. Frequently, communal altars are also constructed, along with these personal ones, in plazas, community centers, and churches, and people are invited to share their pictures of their deceased loved ones. One frequently encounters material objects and letters to the deceased at these altars as well.

While secularization is on the upswing in many Latin American countries, and Protestantism, particularly Pentecostalism,[28] is at-

(Above) A traditional Chinese Buddhist home altar. Note the pictures of both the deceased and various Chinese deities. There are also offerings of fresh food, incense, and candles, which symbolize the ongoing interaction between the living and the dead, the sacred and the profane. Wikipedia Commons *(Below)* A Japanese bone-picking ceremony, traditionally performed by the family following a cremation. Family members place the larger bones into an urn using chopsticks, and then the remaining ashes are placed in the urn along with the bones. In both India and Japan family members are actively involved in the disposal process. Photo by Autumn Snake.

tracting a large percentage of the population (particularly in Brazil), Catholic thought still informs the religious imagination, including many customs of the dead. It is impossible, really, to discuss "Latin America" as though it were a cohesive cultural whole, and clearly the Day of the Dead is peculiar to Mexico, but this close association of the living and the dead stems from the Catholic religious worldview in which saints, martyrs, and the dead can actively intercede for the living at their behest, through their prayers and offerings. Martyrs and saints, in many ways, represent the living dead; they continue to play a role in the realm of the living through active intercession and the answering of prayers. Catholics, because of this practice of praying to martyrs and saints, are generally more accustomed to praying to the dead to intercede for them and help them navigate the living world. Robert Orsi outlines this tendency among urban Italian Catholics in his book, discussing how both the living and the dead affect each other reciprocally through prayer—the living affect the dead who are in purgatory, and the dead help the living navigate their world.[29] The relations between the world of the living and the world of the dead in the Catholic realm are, in this way, similar to those of the Japanese worldview, where the deceased become *kami,* whose function is to help the living and intercede on their behalf. Thus, even in a country like Argentina, which is culturally and geographically removed from Mexico, the Catholic religious imagination plays a large role in the relationship the living have with the dead. Though most Argentines claim to be secular, and many go to church only on major holidays, a surprising the number of them baptize their children and send them to Catholic schools. Uruguay and Chile are similar, as almost all Uruguayans marry in Catholic churches and baptize their children, but only 4 percent actually attend church on a regular basis.[30] The view of death, dying, and the afterlife is thus culturally that of the Catholic religious worldview, in which the dead continue to participate in the lives of the living. My work on martyrdom in Argentina confirms this reality: while I was conducting fieldwork on Carlos Mugica, his sister gave me a piece of the dead priest's bloodied pants and encouraged me to pray to him. Martyrs and saints retain powerful agency through their dead bodies, blood, or other remnants.[31]

Whereas Max Weber may address the effect of Protestant thought on capitalism,[32] it cannot be understated that the Catholic religious imagination regarding the realm of the dead has an enormous influence, and though Protestantism may have laid the foundation for the accumulation of capital, it also seems to have deemphasized the importance of keeping the dead in the realm of the living. The empty cross of Protestantism, which focuses on a theology of salvation, rather than the Passion, contrasts with Catholicism's stress on the importance of the body. It is the missing dead that seem to present challenges in bereavement. Without dead bodies, their agency is missing, and the bereaved are forced to invent new ways of remembering and honoring the dead so that they can continue to be present in the realm of the living. The dead body has been replaced with a figurative rendering of the dead; the bodies and their corporeality are substituted for in some ways by material reminders and virtual images— whether a favorite object of the dead person or an image representing the dead. It is no surprise, then, that Catholicism and, by extension, Catholic countries, for whom the body is so central to a theology of grieving, offer ways of memorializing the dead in an institutional and communally sanctioned way.

Recent Bodiless Memorials: Ghostbikes, Aurora, Nickel Mines, and Sandy Hook

GHOSTBIKES AND THE HAUNTING OF PUBLIC SPACE

Having given a brief overview of bodiless memorials, and an examination of the missing body, I now move to study several recent bodiless memorials in contemporary American culture. Ghostbikes are memorials erected at or near the sites of death of cyclists who died while riding their bikes. Ghostbike memorials are marked with a functional bike that has been spray-painted white; with the bike is a brief history of the cyclist killed, often a picture of the cyclist, and flowers and mementos that accumulate over time.

The practice is believed to have started in St. Louis, Missouri, in 2003, and its aim extends beyond memorialization into the political and popular realms. The website of the organization that

(*Above*) Alicia Frantz's ghostbike; those remembering Alicia dress the bike up in seasonal gear (here Christmas decorations). The bike is under a busy bridge with little foot traffic at 1400 West Division Avenue, near Wicker Park in Chicago. Photo by John Coronado (*Below*) The placard on Alicia Frantz's ghostbike says, "She heard everyday sounds as music," because Alicia was devoted to music and to making recordings out of interesting sounds. See http://ghostbikes .org/alicia-frantz. Photo by John Coronado

promotes the project, www.ghostbike.org, outlines its agenda: to increase driver awareness, to promote cyclist safety, to memorialize those killed, and, most interestingly, to change the ways articles are written that favor the motorist rather than the cyclist. For example, reports of traffic fatalities frequently describe the cyclist as "running into" a car, rather than the cyclist "being hit" by an unobservant driver. The project is interesting because it is a collaboration among cyclists, the organization, and families and friends of those who have been killed. It is a grassroots organization: individuals and bereaved communities use ghostbikes as a recognizable form of memorialization, in a local and personal way. The website lists specific directions for assembling a ghostbike memorial (outlined below), which emphasize the need to lock the bike well to keep it secure. Pictures of the bikes are uploaded to the site (there is a Facebook page as well) according to geographical location, mapped onto a global chart, and linked through webrings for access. In this way, local memorials use global symbols for recognition, operate locally, but are linked to the World Wide Web and given a global community of support. In addition, there are annual and semiannual memorial days, in which communities and cyclists supporting the ghostbike organization come together to clean the bikes, repaint them, and resecure memorials; there are also group rides to raise funds for financial support.

Here is some advice on how [to] make, install and maintain a ghost bike from the NYC Street Memorial Project.
We try to salvage as much material as possible, paying only for paint, a lock, and a chain, with a total cost of maybe $25–$50 per memorial.

How to Obtain and Prepare a Bike:
We usually get free "junk" bike donations from bike repair shops or local supporters. We strip each bike of non-essential parts (cables, grips, brakes) and recycle them; this makes it easier to paint and also less attractive to thieves. You should probably use a bike that does not have sentimental value because it could be removed. . . .

How to Paint a Ghost Bike:
There is a very detailed guide to painting bikes at WikiHow, but
the basics are:

• Degrease & clean the bike before painting;
• Apply 1 coat of primer (2 coats on tires, seat, and any rusty
areas);
• Apply 1 to 2 coats of flat white spray paint evenly from all
angles;
• Let dry for 24 hours before handling or installing.
   One or two ghost bikes have been painted in colors other than
white.
   In NYC we hold ghost bike workdays inviting everyone to help
with making and installing ghost bikes. This is a great way to get
new volunteers involved in a ghost bike project and to connect
with the friends and family of cyclists killed. . . .

How to Install a Ghost Bike:
 In NYC, it is our experience that a ghost bike has the best chance
of staying installed if it is locked well; try to lock both wheels. We
lock the bike in place just as if it was a functioning bike. It is also
a good idea to be sure it is not blocking pedestrian, bike or car
passage nor locked to any public works (ie: street lights), trees,
parks or private property (unless you get permission). A street sign
is usually the best choice even if it isn't exactly where the crash
took place. Some groups have placed ghost bikes above street
signs and encased the wheels in cement. Keep in mind that if you
ride or wheel the bike to its destination you are likely to wear the
paint off its tires; it's better to carry it or bring it on a bike trailer,
car or public transport.[33]

Several interesting aspects surround these ghostbike projects: they
are started at the grassroots level, they are creating memorials out of
new or donated materials, they are appropriating aspects of popular
culture (ghosts) to make their symbolism understood rather than using the bikes involved in the accidents, and they are using public
space for private memorialization. The first ghostbike seems to date

to 2003, on Holly Hills Lane in St. Louis, after Patrick Van Der Tuin
saw a cyclist killed by a motorist in a bike lane. Van Der Tuin left a
white painted bike at the spot of the accident with a sign that read,
"Cyclist Struck Here." Not long after, Van Der Tuin solicited the help
of friends and placed more bikes throughout St. Louis, in other dangerous spots for cyclists, to generate cycle awareness and safety. Not
long after, other U.S. cities followed suit (Pittsburgh, New York City,
Seattle, and Chicago among them), in addition to other countries.

Ghostbikes are usually pristine and white, phantomlike presenc-
es on street corners meant to warn of dangerous intersections and
careless drivers. The bikes are almost always functioning (though often secondhand), rather than the remnants of a biking accident. They
use the popular and universal image of ghosts to make their point—
and though some ghostbikes have been painted other colors, almost
all of them are a stark and ghostly white. This is not merely a replacement of the cyclist, an apparition of the missing body and his or her
bike in the afterlife, but it is also a reminder of the bike before its
rider's death—a bike before its fateful collision. The bike—like the
body—is presented as clean and pristine; there is no evidence of the
terrible effects of the car accident on the bike itself. It is, essentially, a
memorial made digestible for the American public—powerful yet
presentable.[34]

These ghostbikes, though, are not always welcome additions to
the (usually) urban landscape, evidenced both by the ghostbike website's emphasis on locking the bikes (or even placing the wheels in cement) and by various protests against the placement of ghostbikes in
public spaces.[35] One famous example is the protest in Dupont Circle,
in Washington, D.C. Alice Swanson was killed on her bike at the intersection of Connecticut Avenue and R and 20th Streets Northwest
by a garbage truck in 2008, after which Swanson's family and friends
installed a ghostbike in her memory. The district's Department of
Public Works then removed the ghostbike memorial in 2009 at the
mayor's request because of the district's policy of removing all memorials in public spaces within thirty days. A few months later, the
ghostbike community installed twenty-two bikes, one for each year
of Swanson's life, at the same intersection; these were soon removed.
Finally, one more attempt was made, as another single ghostbike was

installed at the same intersection, and this time it was allowed to stay, locked to a lamppost in full public view.

The battle between Swanson's family and friends and the District of Columbia underscores an important aspect of memorialization, one that is highlighted in many studies conducted on roadside memorialization: the tension between those who seek to memorialize in a personal and private way in a public space and those who are guardians of these public spaces. As Clark and Franzmann explain, "How can an individual or a small group, such as a family or, as is often the case, a group of school friends, reclaim public, secular space as a significant place? Perhaps by demonstrating an emotional and spiritual connection with that space and marking it with the symbolic white cross so that it must draw respect. The roadside memorial can represent an act of reclamation."[36] That reclamation, however, occurs in the public sphere and in secular space; reclaiming by those memorializing is sometimes seen as inconvenient and troublesome by those whose encounter with these memorials in their everyday space becomes problematic. Though the state (or, in this case, the city) seeks to intervene (the excuse in the Swanson ghostbike removal was that the bike "was an eyesore") and reclaim these spaces, the memorializers often use what they believe to be a moral authority to claim the public space as their own.[37] Memorials such as the ghostbike memorials thus become intersections of the sacred and secular, the private and public, reinscribing and remapping meaning into everyday topographies, and not always in comfortable and acceptable ways.

Mapping Memorials on Public Spaces: Aurora, Colorado

The July 20, 2012, shootings at the Batman movie *The Dark Knight Rises* in Aurora, Colorado, in which twelve people were killed and another fifty-eight injured is another example of the tensions of personal versus public space. It is also another example of grassroots memorialization occurring at the spot of death rather than at the site of the bodies themselves. Shortly after the senseless rampage by a gunman against moviegoers at the midnight showing at Century Aurora 16 theater, a memorial emerged across the street, in which the deaths of the twelve killed were remembered with white crosses and hundreds of material offerings, including flowers, balloons, letters, candles, and stuffed animals (the youngest of those killed was a six-year-old girl). The most interesting aspect of this memorial was its connection to the Columbine killings nearly twenty years earlier, as the memorial crosses erected at the site were constructed by the same builder. Greg Zanis, the son of a Greek Orthodox priest and founder of the organization Crosses for Losses, first started building crosses after his father-in-law and best friend were murdered. A part-time carpenter, Zanis found meaning in building and erecting crosses in their memory, and he built the large, twelve-foot crosses at the site of the Columbine shootings. Zanis first became known for the controversy surrounding the crosses because he originally built and erected fifteen crosses at Columbine, thirteen for the victims and two for the gunmen themselves.[38] The father of one victim tore down the two crosses for the young gunmen and angrily criticized Zanis for even wanting to build crosses in their memory.

Zanis has continued to create controversy, erecting crosses for Lisa Stebic, who as of this writing has not been officially declared dead, and then again at the scene of the Windy City Core Supply murders, whose victims included a Muslim and a Jew.[39] Zanis does not take money for his efforts, and he claims that he builds his memorial crosses only for those for whom he receives personal requests; he estimates the number of crosses that he has personally built and erected at over three thousand. His memorials thus are unique in that he is, as an individual, driving much of American memorialization, or at least, the way it looks and is constructed. He generally uses all wood, making crosses that range from three feet, like those at the Aurora memorial, to twelve feet, like those at the Columbine memorial. The crosses are all painted a simple white and placed far enough apart that material memorials may be left at their feet and yet be distinguished from one another. In a way, Zanis is a performance artist, whose work is unique to a particular genre of American popular memorialization.[40] The crosses, like the ghostbikes painted white, are ghostly apparitions in a natural landscape and serve as stand-ins for corpses, pristine and clean. Additionally, because Zanis always uses crosses, they are uniquely religious symbols used to impart sacredness to public and secular land. The Aurora memorial, across the street from the cinema, was in the direct line of sight from the movie theater where the killings took place. It emerged somewhat spontaneously in that location, but once Zanis constructed his crosses (he erected them there on July 22, two days following the shooting), the memorial was a communally recognized location of grief for both the survivors and the bereaved.

The memorial was allowed to stay there until September 20, 2012, two months after the shootings took place. The city decided to remove the memorial and gave the grieving families a couple of weeks' notice that the memorial would be taken down, offering them the option of helping with the removal of the memorial, which only a few of the families chose to do. The memorial artifacts were then bagged and filed, to be kept for the local museum. The items from the memorial, not including the many stuffed animals, which were given to local charities for children, filled more than 160 boxes. The *Denver Post* quotes local officials responsible for the removal of the memorial: "Aaron B. Gagné, manager of Aurora's Neighborhood Services department, said that if family members want to, they can visit the warehouse and pore over items left to honor their loved ones. 'They'll be able to come in and sit down in a conference room and go through these items,' Gagné said. 'There will be ongoing opportunities to do this.'"[41] The memorial artifacts will eventually be catalogued and curated into a show for the Aurora History Museum.[42]

Cinemark, which owns the Century Aurora 16 theater, reopened the theater on January 17, inviting the bereaved families to a night of remembrance, as part of the dedication ceremony. Cinemark did not anticipate the outrage that followed, as many described the event as distasteful; nine of the twelve victims' families wrote to Cinemark and called for a boycott of the theater.[43] The letter read, "During the holiday we didn't think anyone or anything could make our grief worse but you, Cinemark, have managed to do just that by sending us an invitation two days after Christmas inviting us to attend the reopening of your theater in Aurora where our loved ones were massacred."[44] It is interesting that the memorial across the street, with its white crosses in an open landscape, was deemed acceptable, though memorial remembrance at the cinema, the actual site of the deaths, was deemed distasteful and was so vehemently criticized. If anything, the memorial inside the cinema brings the spectacle of death closer, whereas the memorial outside is farther removed from both the bodies and the site of death. Not all were against the theater's actions, however: Steve Hogan, Aurora's mayor, spoke out in favor of the event: "We are a community that is united in our recovery. The reopening of this theater is part of that recovery process." He went on: "Not everyone scarred by what happened wanted to be here. That is a valid choice and we will respect that choice. But everyone here now also made an equally valid choice. And my personal choice is to be here. I cannot allow the shooter, in any way, shape or form, to win."[45]

Several issues are important to note regarding the Aurora memorial. First is the effect that Greg Zanis has in creating and contributing to "spontaneous" memorialization. While much has been made of spontaneous memorialization, it is important to note the role of certain individuals, such as Zanis, in this trend. Zanis's crosses are recognizable symbols of contemporary American memorialization; they have become so through the use of Christian religious imagery, familiar signifiers of other memorials of mass shootings. Zanis's contribution immediately increased news coverage and visibility for the Aurora shootings, as he personally made the crosses, driving to Colorado from Illinois almost immediately upon hearing about the shootings and installing the crosses himself, thereby linking the events in Aurora with those nearly twenty years earlier in Columbine. With Zanis's contributions, memorialization is seen not merely as a popular and spontaneous trend, but as one that is intentionally and individually driven as well.[46] Additionally, the mayor of Aurora and President Obama himself visited the site within days, lending the memorial some credibility and ensuring its "official" status as a nationally recognized site of mourning. Second, though, are the limits placed on the memorial in both time and space by the city. The mayor visited the site almost immediately to demonstrate his solidarity with the memorialization project, but he also is the one who urged the community to move forward through (1) the removal of the memorial; (2) the cataloguing and shelving of the material artifacts at the memorial site, which would become part of a future curated show at the local history museum; and (3) the reopening six months later of the movie theater where the shootings took place. Removing the memorial and cataloguing its items for a future chapter of Aurora's history are a manipulation of public space whereby its purpose is shifted from the personal and private to the public and civic. The place is reclaimed as secular space, but even its private memorial objects are considered no longer personal but communal—part of the community's historical narrative and broader story. The mayor frames the experience of the reopening and dedication of the movie theater as a positive one—a moving forward and a healing. By his doing this, space is reclaimed as part of the public and civic sphere. Time also is appropriated; moving forward is seen not as moving on but as healing, and memorial artifacts are now a part of the community's past. The Aurora memorial manipulated bodies, space, and time—bodies reimagined in landscapes through crosses, and space and time shifting in tension with one another, the local authorities carefully ensuring that both space and time returned to their previous states.

Mapping Memorials in Public Spaces: Nickel Mines and Sandy Hook

Like Columbine and Aurora, Nickel Mines and Sandy Hook are also strangely related to one another: both are communities that suffered horrendous and unimaginable losses: the mass shooting and killing of elementary school children by a single mass murderer. But the communal response and memorialization of the two events have been very different. The Nickel Mines tragedy occurred on October 2, 2006, in Lancaster County, Pennsylvania, when Charles Carl Roberts IV entered the local one-room schoolhouse and shot ten young Amish girls, killing five, in supposed retribution for the death of his young newborn girl. Roberts then killed himself inside the schoolhouse once he realized police had surrounded the schoolhouse. Following the shooting, funerals for the five girls were held in the traditional Amish style, but the community stunned the outside world with their treatment of the killer's family. Within hours of the shooting, the Amish visited the houses of Roberts's parents, in-laws, and wife and children, offering their condolences over the loss of their son, expressing deep remorse, and letting the parents know that they shared their loss. Additionally, Roberts's wife was one of the few non-Amish invited to the funeral of one of the young girls. These simple gestures shocked the world and truly seemed at odds with the reactions, for example, of the victims' families at Columbine, where one of the fathers tore down the crosses memorializing the Columbine killers.

Even more interesting, though, was the lack of memorialization, which many non-Amish sought to do in remembrance of the five girls who had died. Within ten days of the shooting, the school building was razed so that a new school building could be built in its place. Some wanted to transform the school building into a memorial, but the Amish did not want to bring even more tourists into the area, particularly for such a reason. They chose, rather, to destroy the building and erect a new one in which to conduct their lessons. No memorial would be built at Nickel Mines, except for five trees planted in the young girls' honor. An article in the *Huffington Post* captured this event beautifully, explaining the religious symbolism in both the refusal to memorialize and the planting of the trees:

> Beyond the practical reasons, however, were deep religious beliefs that guided the decision not to construct a memorial. The Amish eschew set-apart sacred places and buildings—even churches. They hold worship services in their homes as a testament to their convictions that daily life should blend with religious experience. Religious shrines, they fear, will divert their spiritual affections away from God and toward the humanly constructed artifacts. Constructed monuments, in their view, accentuate the artistic skill of the designers and architects, rather than the deeper meaning of the historical events. . . .
>
> A few old trees remain standing in the pasture that had been the schoolyard. In addition, five young evergreens now grow along a nearby fence row. They stand unnoticed to visitors driving along White Oak Road. They rise heavenward, quietly pointing to the Divine Grace that somehow enabled the community to forgive within hours of the violence. They remain green even in winter— fitting memorials that recall not the violence but the grace of that

awful day. And the neighbors who travel White Oak Road, Amish and non-Amish alike, see them and remember.[47]

Part of the reason for the lack of memorialization is the treatment given to the dead bodies following the shootings. There is some variation among Amish communities regarding the treatment of the body and funeral services, but the Amish in Lancaster County usually follow certain traditions regarding the disposal of the corpse. Because the Amish there are "house Amish," they do not have a church in which to hold a church service or a funeral. There are other American Amish communities that have churches and therefore might hold a funeral in one. Generally, among Lancaster Amish, when someone dies, the body is first taken home, where it is washed and cared for, then given to the care of a local undertaker to be embalmed. Embalmment for the Amish community is handled by one of Lancaster County's few funeral homes and is done according to strict Amish customs: the body is embalmed to prevent putrefaction only, but makeup, hair dyes, and other cosmetics are not permitted. Following embalmment, the body is dressed in white long underwear and returned to the family to be clothed. Women traditionally dress a female corpse in a white dress, cape, and apron, and male corpses are dressed by men in a white vest, pants, and shirt. Family members are actively involved in the preparation of the corpse for burial, and they then host a wake in their own home. The funeral ceremony generally takes place three days following the death, and thus the wake occurs rather quickly, usually on the second day. Funeral attendees generally wear black, and corpses are buried in the ground in one of Lancaster's twenty Amish cemeteries in a wooden coffin that is tapered at both ends and wider in the middle. The funeral services are held in the home itself, and the minister generally gives a short religious sermon, after which the body is carried in the family's buggy to the grave itself, where the Lord's Prayer is silently said over the coffin and the corpse is buried.

The bodies of the girls who died in the Nickel Mines shooting, then, were very much present for their families and the Amish community. The need to memorialize through a replacement of the body did not exist, as the families were actively involved in the preparation of the corpses for burial and in the funeral service itself. Additionally, the theological understanding of the body, and its role in both death and the afterlife, helped locate the bodies firmly within the community and the church. Nickel Mines has no constructed memorial, nor is there a dislocation of either body or place.[48] The wake and funeral, both held in the home, firmly locate death in the home, the same place life is lived—which is not unlike the tradition of Japanese Buddhists and American funerary traditions of 150 years ago. There is essentially no separation from the corpse or the remembering of the dead; both occur in the realm of the living.[49]

Like those at Nickel Mines, the shootings at Sandy Hook Elementary School in Newtown, Connecticut, involved the shooting and killing of young elementary school children. On December 14, 2012, Adam Lanza shot and killed his mother and then drove to Sandy Hook Elementary School, where he proceeded to kill twenty young children and six staff members before turning the gun on himself and committing suicide. By that evening, both President Obama and Connecticut's Governor Dan Malloy had addressed the incident, Obama using the event as a political platform, criticizing lax gun control laws,[50] and Malloy speaking about moving forward. Malloy said, "Evil visited this community today, and it is too early to speak of recovery, but each parent, each sibling, each member of the family has to understand that Connecticut, we are all in this together, we will do whatever we can to overcome this event, we will get through it."[51]

Memorialization occurred quickly for the Sandy Hook victims, as spontaneous memorials emerged in all sorts of places and in all forms. Memorials were erected at the site of the shootings, at various churches, in people's yards, and in public places such as street corners and central Newtown buildings. Memorials consisted of candles, teddy bears, balloons, flowers, and various other offerings, including more-personalized memorials such as flags, on the stripes of which were written the names of the twenty-six victims, wooden angels mounted in the ground, each bearing personal characteristics of skin and hair color to symbolize a specific victim, roses imprinted with a picture of each of the victims on the outer petals, and so on. Even Greg Zanis erected yet another memorial here in Newtown, though

Newtown's memorial emerged spontaneously and organically; an outpouring of emotion was reflected in child-oriented memorializations: balloons, flowers, and thousands of stuffed animals, especially teddy bears, were left at various sites throughout Newtown. The shootings occurred in the middle of winter, and city officials were faced with the logistical issue of keeping the memorial objects clean, dry, and out of the way—hence the tents. Creative Commons

his four-foot-high white crosses were not the central memorial image captured on film. (The angels tended to be the most popular representations of the slain victims.)[52]

In contrast to the Nickel Mines shootings, those at Sandy Hook revealed a rapid and enormous memorialization response, one mirrored throughout communities in the United States. It was, in some ways, the closest trend in memorialization to the events after 9/11, in both scope and response. Like those in Aurora, however, officials curtailed the memorialization, but in this instance, rather than allowing two months, it was removed after two weeks. Again the decision to break down the spontaneous memorials was made in the name of "moving forward" and "healing" the community; there were also official concerns regarding the integrity of the memorials, as snow, rain, and the natural elements made the makeshift memorials an eyesore to some in the community. The *New York Times* reported the official response of Newtown to the memorials:

> Patricia Llodra, Newtown's first selectwoman, made the painful decision for many herself when she ordered the Public Works Department two weeks after the shooting to remove many of the most elaborate memorials. To be removed were the vast gardens of grief—including rows of decorated Christmas trees topped with silken angels, green and white balloons (the school's colors), sacrificial candles and deeply personal items like old dolls and sports trophies—that had accumulated outside the firehouse near the school and in the center of Sandy Hook. . . .
>   That night, after most of the town had gone to bed, employees from the Public Works Department collected all the material, placed it in containers and took it to the department's warehouse. Ms. Llodra has invited everyone to take their memorials to the department for inclusion in the permanent memorial. "There's no road map for this," Ms. Llodra said. "So I have to really make the decisions based on what my heart tells me is right and what my head says is possible. . . . And after being weathered . . . I mean, we had bad rain, we had a storm, we had wind, we had snow. So I knew the time was going to come where we really had to move the memorials. Not only because the tributes themselves start to look unkempt and start to communicate a message that wasn't part of the honoring that the donor intended; it also signifies a moving on, a readiness for the community to go to that next step."[53]

Though memorials in Newtown's public spaces were taken down on December 28, 2012, some preferred to keep their memorials up on their own private property, most often saying that they were not yet ready to take down the memorials, and that it was still "too soon."[54] Newtown's memorials were much more numerous than Aurora's single memorial, which was located on the outskirts of town, across from the movie theater; concerns regarding traffic flow and the sheer volume of memorialization in Newtown are understandable, but the response nevertheless seems rather fast. The solution to the proliferation of memorial materials in Newtown is similar to that of Aurora:

the removal of materials to an official and state-sponsored memorial that can be neatly framed, categorized, and contained. But there is an extent to which these events can occur at the popular level before they must be reined in by the state. Newtown city officials wrote letters to the survivors of the victims, purportedly including them in the process of removing and cataloguing the memorials. The message here is clear: memorials are allowed, but only for a limited time in public (and political) space. Sara Mosle, in her article "The Lives Unlived in Newtown," in the *New York Times Magazine,* compared the memorialization in Newtown to that after another elementary school tragedy in New London, Texas, writing that a memorial service scheduled to be held a year after the deaths was canceled because at that time it was still too soon to mourn and put closure on the event. The time difference between these two events is striking: the Newtown memorial was taken down after two weeks for the purpose of "moving on," whereas in 1937, even after a year, the community in Texas considered it too soon to move forward and heal.[55] When memorials are taken out of the public sphere, the message is clear: memorials prevent us from moving forward and healing, from "a return to normalcy." Through the manipulation of public space—returning private memorialization to the private realm and reclaiming public space—time itself is being manipulated.

Grief, however, is not something that can be rushed, and the classification of grief as something to *move beyond,* rather than a state to be *lived in,* is precisely the problem. Laura Tanner writes, "The continued dominance of Freud's influential theory of mourning demonstrates not only a cultural injunction to move through grief but a tendency to define bereavement and its consolations in symbolic terms that obscure the bodily dimensions of loss."[56] In less than a hundred years, grief as a process has been whittled down; at one time a year was not enough to grieve properly, now two months or even two weeks is considered enough time. With the disappearance from the public realm of both dead bodies and the memorials that honor them, grief itself has been displaced. Bodiless memorials function as substitutions for the corpse—ways in which we attempt to keep the dead in the realm of the living. When we disappear the corpse through embalmment or cremation, and then again banish the corpse from our home to the funeral home, we lose the dead, but this loss is multiplied when we also lose the memorials that function to remember the dead—the memorials in place of bodies that live among the living.

2

Wearing the Dead

Wearing Our Mourning

The development of tattooing is one way to carry the dead around with us, while also making the status of the bereaved clearly evident to those around them. Tattooing is a visual marker that concretely indicates one's status as bereaved to the community, by memorializing the dead through the inscribing of names, images, or even replicas of body parts (such as handprints or footprints of the deceased) on living bodies. Tattoo remembrances are literally carried with us, age with us, and allow a virtual afterlife for the dead, simultaneously establishing the identity of the bereaved in a fixed and permanent way in a society that denies the corpse and no longer gives space for grieving. Here we move from the missing dead body to the practice of using living bodies to recover the dead.

A Brief Global History of Tattooing

Tattooing has a long history, cycling through social acceptance, revulsion, and indifference. Though many histories put the popularity of the modern practices of tattooing as originating in Polynesia,[1] it has been around since the beginnings of humankind; the first evidence of tattooing was found on the frozen remains of a Neolithic man discovered in 1991 in the Italian Alps.[2] Greek and Roman histories, however, provide the first extant records of tattoos as a means of control, employed by the state to coerce, control, and stigmatize people. Most recently, the Nazi regime employed this device in World War II with Jews and other prisoners held captive in concentration camps. Through the association of tattoos with slaves or criminals, the state's use of tattooing to exert control over the body is one of the ways that tattoos historically became associated with marginal society. It is also among the Greeks and Romans that the practice of tattoo removal first seems to have emerged—the attempt to erase the state-enforced marginal status of those tattooed.[3]

In the modern West, tattooing has traditionally been associated with marginal society—the lower and working classes, soldiers, convicts, motorcycle gangs, and circus performers—but this is a skewed understanding if one looks at the history of tattooing in its entirety. In Victorian times tattooing gained popularity in upper-crust society, among women in particular, as they tattooed their lips as a marker of status.[4] This identification of tattooing with status is once again emerging among today's American middle class. An association between celebrities and tattoos first became apparent in the 1990s. Tattooing in American culture today is so commonplace that children receive temporary tattoos in their goodie bags at birthday parties, *Sesame Street* featured tattoos in a show, and there is even a Tattoo Barbie.[5] In short, tattoos are one of the markers of belonging to a middle-class suburban culture with a discretionary income. Today one in four Americans has a tattoo,[6] and among American youth ages eighteen to twenty-nine, nearly 40 percent have at least one tattoo.[7] American youth subculture has rescued tattooing from its most recent marginal status, though part of its appeal to youths might in fact be its marginality, so it remains to be seen whether tattooing will continue to enjoy its recent comeback in mainstream society.

In China tattooing was also traditionally practiced among marginal peoples and, as occurred in the Greco-Roman period in the West, was sometimes used as a way to enforce status and class differences. Criminals, prostitutes, and those among the lower classes in China often underwent punitive tattooing as a way to easily identify their lower status at city gates. Tattooing enjoyed a brief surge of popularity, however, with the portrayal of tattooed bandits in a famous Chinese classic novel, *The Water Margins,* or *Shui Hu Zhuan.*[8] The novel is based on a true story of bandits active during the Song Dynasty; the thieves were colorful characters whose tattoos were as illustrious as their characters. When *The Water Margins* emerged in popular Chinese culture in fourteenth-century China, tattooing briefly became popular among the literary elite, but it eventually returned to its marginal status, where it remained until very recently.[9] Today in China tattooing is still associated mostly with criminals[10] and those on the margins of Chinese society, such as the ethnic minorities of the Lis in Hainan and the Dulong in Yunnan.[11]

In Japan tattoos were traditionally associated with marginal characters, from geishas to samurai to *yakuza* (loosely translated as organized crime) to lower-class workers. Tattoos in Japan were a visual hallmark of one's marginal status, but they also served as a symbol of self-imposed exclusion, which was widely recognized and celebrated in these marginal groups. The stigma of tattoos in Japan is still prevalent today; one may not enter a traditional bathhouse, hot springs, or even a water park if one's skin is tattooed (a stigma similar to the taboo on tattoos in the workplace in the United States). These practices are changing under the influence of modernization and the effects of the global economy, as tattoos become a feature of Western youth culture, and Japanese youths import this popular trend as they begin to reject traditional attitudes toward tattoos.[12]

On the other hand, in Polynesia, Micronesia, and New Zealand, tattooing has served as a way of marking one's clan identification and has been used as a way of displaying—in an obvious and literal form—rites of passage from childhood into adulthood. One's markings tell the world who one is and define one's position within society. In Samoa, for example, it was common practice for men to have a *pe'a* tattooed on the body, a black tattoo inked in a traditional geometric design, reaching from just above the knees to above the groin and buttocks area. Boys who received these tattoos were considered brave (and able to afford them; they were very expensive, and the tattoo artist often received many hundreds of mats in exchange for his work). Boys who did not receive them were known as *telenoa,* or naked. The basis of tattoos in Samoa is clear: they are both markers of status and indicators of personal character.[13] Tattoo memorials were also inscribed among the Polynesian peoples; the most popular example is the Hawaiian queen Kamamalu. When her mother-in-law died in the 1820s, Queen Kamamalu had her tongue tattooed in remembrance. Legend has it that the "missionary William Ellis watched the procedure, commenting to the queen that she must be undergoing great pain. The queen replied, He eha nui no, he nui roa ra ku'u aroha. (Great pain indeed, greater is my affection.)"[14] Tattooing in the Pacific islands thus was practiced by both men and women, as markers of clan identity and status, and it seems to have naturally segued into the custom of tattoo memorialization for the dead.

Tattooing also has a long history in Latin America; complex tattoo designs have been found on Latin American mummies dating from the eleventh century in pre-Incan Peru. Both men and women in Latin America practiced tattooing, and the Jesuit missionary Martin Dobrizhoffer observed tattooing in the eighteenth century as a common practice during his work with the Guarani and the Abipones. Associated with the indigenous tribes of Latin America in the Chacos and near the Amazon, traditional tattooing has recently been supplemented by other styles of tattooing. Tattoos in Latin America thus range from traditional tribal tattoos associated with indigenous peoples to Western- and Japanese-style "piece" tattoos worn as emblems of upper-middle-class youth, which are replete with images of a global middle-class pop culture (as opposed to tribal markings). In more recent years, tattoos have grown in popularity, particularly among the upper-middle-class youth and intelligentsia. Tattooing still has a somewhat marginal quality in Latin America, though, as it is very expensive, seen as a by-product of traditional indigenous culture, and becoming associated with an alternative youth subculture. Tattooing, while growing in popularity in Latin America, is not nearly as mainstream as tattooing in the United States.

Globalization of Tattoos

Around the world, tattooing, whether a marker of social acceptance or rejection, marginality or high status and acceptance, has historically been a way by which people can map their place in society through the canvas of their skin. Tattoos thus serve as geographic maps of the world and permanent timelines by marking rites of passage, important events, people, and even memories, all literally inscribed on a living canvas that actively interacts with the world around it. As globalization becomes widespread, tattoos can no longer be strictly associated with their individual cultural and historical genealogies; rather, the modern-day tattoo may have many cultural associations and meanings attached to it—adaptations of various cultural implications inscribed on a canvas that the individual assembles as her or his own genealogical map. This is why, in examining the rising trend of tattoo memorials, the history of tattooing must be viewed within a global context. Tattoos may symbolize rejection in one culture, while signifying acceptance in another, and we must be careful not to read tattoos in one cultural language.

Tattooing in the Religious Realm

Tattoos play an important role in the religious realm as well. Either in their acceptance and promotion or in their forbiddance, most religions have very clear-cut ideas about the role and importance of tattoos. Tattoos can be the locus of the sacred revealed in and on the flesh, or they can be markings of the emphasis placed on the material over and above the spiritual. In the Jewish and Christian worldviews, the Bible is very clear about tattoos. Leviticus 19:28 addresses the practice of tattooing: "You shall not make any gashes in your flesh for the dead or tattoo any marks upon you: I am the Lord."[15] Some branches of Judaism and Christianity have pointed to this passage as a proscription against tattoos; however, what is important here is the linking of the practice of tattooing with mourning. This passage clearly reveals that the practice of engraving one's status as mourner on one's body is a practice that finds its roots in ancient society.[16] In revisiting this passage, one must wonder if it forbids tattooing itself or the practice of inscribing tattoo memorials on one's body. This is beyond the scope of this chapter; regardless, it is clear that tattoo memorials were common enough that the religious leaders of the time outlawed their continuance.

Some Jews believe that one cannot be buried in Jewish grounds if one is tattooed. This proscription of tattooing is part of the deep shame and resentment imposed on the Jews during the Holocaust, when the Nazi regime tattooed (actually, branded) its prisoners, knowing the Jewish ban on tattooing of the body (and may be in part why modern cemeteries have not been completely strict in enforcing this rule).[17] Recently, however, a handful of Jewish descendants of

Holocaust victims have started the practice of tattooing their parents' and, more often, grandparents' numbers on their own forearms out of respect and the desire to remember the Holocaust in a way that is forever embedded not only in their memories, but also on their skins. The dominant discourse forbidding the practice still prevails, though the few instances of tattooing as a form of remembrance challenge this taboo.[18]

Similarly, in Islam tattoos are forbidden because they are considered an alteration of Allah's most perfect creature. That being said, one who has tattoos may be able to convert to Islam, but one must first promise not to get any more tattoos. Tattooing itself is considered *haraam*, or a major sin in Islam; thus, tattoo memorials and tattooing do not generally exist in Muslim countries.[19] The Hadith, which is the complementary text to the Qur'an and is widely used to interpret and understand the Qur'an (much like the Talmud for Judaism), is very clear on its proscription of tattooing. The Hadith contains many references to the prohibition of tattooing, and the specific textual references are against both tattooing and tattooing as a tool for beautification. Two of the many examples from different Hadith authors follow.

Abu Dawud Book 028, Hadith Number 4157.

Narrated By 'Abd Allah b. Mas'ud: Allah has cursed the woman who tattoos and the women who have themselves tattooed, the women who add false hair (according to the version of Muhammad b. Isa) and the women who pluck hair from their faces (according to the version of 'Uthman). The agreed version then goes: the women who make spaces between teeth for beauty, changing what Allah has created.

Sahih Bukhari Volume 003, Book 034, Hadith Number 440.

Narrated By Aun bin Abu Juhaifa: I saw my father buying a slave whose profession was cupping, and ordered that his instruments (of cupping) be broken. I asked him the reason for doing so. He replied, "Allah's Apostle prohibited taking money for blood, the price of a dog, and the earnings of a slave-girl by prostitution; he

cursed her who tattoos and her who gets tattooed, the eater of
Riba (usury), and the maker of pictures."[20]

Here we see the prohibition not only of tattoos, but also of those who
give tattoos and of the use of tattooing to "improve" one's appear-
ance, on the basis that God creates his creatures in his image, and
therefore they are perfect and should not be altered.

Hinduism has no stance, either for or against tattoos, as long as
the tattoos are not disrespectful to a particular deity or person. One
particular sect, however, famously practices full-body tattooing, inking the name of Ram all over the body. The practice started in the
nineteenth century, when local Brahmins persecuted a group of untouchables because they were practicing Brahmanic rites. To protect
themselves, the untouchables tattooed the name of Ram all over their
bodies, preventing the Brahmins from taking out their wrath on their
bodies. The practice persisted, and today these tattooed men are
known as Ramnamis, though their numbers are now dwindling.[21]
Similarly, Buddhism has no particular position on tattoos, though
there is a proscription against the intentional harming of the body,
and some interpret tattooing to fall in this category. Lay Buddhists
are much more prone to seek tattoos, though, than Buddhist monks
and priests, and more recently Thailand has sought to ban foreign
tourists from seeking tattoos with a Buddhist theme, as Thais feel
that foreigners don't always understand or respect the meaning behind Buddhist images and inscriptions.[22] It seems that only the mono-
theistic traditions have a specific text-based bias against tattoos,
though culturally tattoos have cycled in and out of favor in Asian traditions such as Buddhism and Hinduism.

Wearing the Dead: Tattoo Memorials in Contemporary Society

Having given a brief global history of tattooing, including various
religious attitudes, I now turn to the practice of tattoo memorials,
which seem to have become more and more popular in several contemporary cultures. Though skin is difficult to preserve, and thus the
history of tattoo memorials is difficult to trace, tattoo memorializa-

tion has been practiced for at least several thousand years. One must ask, then, why tattoo memorialization is reemerging as a popular practice in contemporary pop culture. Why are people memorializing the dead as a constant reminder on their skin, rather than leaving the dead in their burial plots or their urns? Tattoo parlors are seeing their business buoyed by memorial tattoos; some tattoo parlor owners state that anywhere from 30 to 40 percent of their tattoos are actually memorials to loved ones who have died.[23]

Common memorial subjects of the tattoos are names of the deceased, pictures of the deceased, handprints or footprints of the deceased (this seems to be a more common practice for memorializing deceased infants and children),[24] or symbolic representations of the dead through imagery typically associated with that individual. Religious imagery ranges from angels and skulls (usually influenced in part by ethnic and cultural background; skulls are common and affectionate ways to represent deceased loved ones in Latin America,

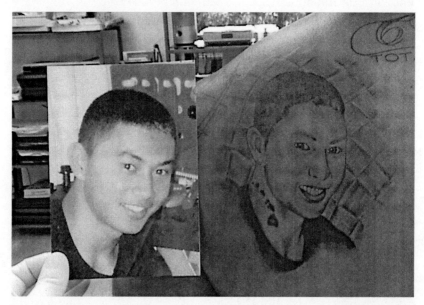

This tattoo was inked by Shane (of Eastside Tattoo) on a father whose son (depicted) had died. The father requested a tattoo of his son, but see the addition of a Hawaiian Islands tattoo on the son's neck. The son had always wanted this particular tattoo, so Shane gave the son a postmortem one. Thus, the tattoo is not only a memorial, but also a way in which the father can give his son the tattoo that he had wanted. Photo by Shane (Eastside Tattoo)

particularly in Mexico, as they have an association with the traditional celebration of the Day of the Dead, whereas skulls are considered macabre in Western European countries) to butterflies, birds,
poetry, flowers, and religious verse. Tattoo memorials also vary by
gender; men often tend toward more "masculine" imagery or literal
depictions of the deceased, while women often memorialize in sentimental ways or with poetry. The imagery and messages inked in tattoo memorials, however, may reveal as much about the choices
available to the person receiving the tattoo as about that person himself or herself. In other words, though tattoos may be becoming more
commonplace, the tattoo wearer operates within a society that accepts, promotes, and rejects particular symbols, images, and depictions in the remembrance of the dead. In addition, often these symbols
are framed along gender lines, and the tattoo wearer may consciously
or unconsciously feel some need to acquiesce to these societal standards, especially if the tattoo is to fit within the syntax of memorialization on skin.

Imprints of the Dead: Grieving Babies and Children through Tattoos

One example of this gendered tattooing is a young Catholic woman,
Donna G., who had three miscarriages, in addition to her two living
children. She chose to bury the fetuses of her miscarriages in her
backyard, but she also wanted a tribute to her three miscarried children, and she tattooed a small cherub on her arm for each of her
losses. The cherubs surround the names of her two living children
and represent, for her, the hope that these three lost children are protecting her two living children. She feels that tattooing the miscarried
babies as angels demonstrates a respect and love for the lives she
wants to commemorate. Additionally, though, this tattoo serves as a
memory of a particularly painful time, while still a celebration of her
children who survived. She says, "They are always with me. I won't
ever forget them."[25] Additionally, though, the tattoo maps her own
particular loss, reflecting the sorrow that she carries with her, in a
way that is recognizable and translatable into everyday discourse.
Angels illustrate the religious imagery available to Donna as an ob-

servant Latin-rite Catholic and give physical form (in a permanent cherubic state) to the fetuses she miscarried; for Donna it is clear that these three losses represent children who are part of her permanent landscape of loss, and she wants to give them a place in her world by placing them next to her surviving children. Donna's choice of imagery is cloaked in religious iconography, which clearly maps her religious beliefs on her skin in a way that is both religiously and socially acceptable. For Donna, these miscarriages were children, and not merely fetuses, and placing her surviving children's names on her skin among the images of the angels helps emphasize that point. It also gives Donna a way in which to acknowledge her losses in a physical and socially recognizable way. While she "wears" her children as angels on her arm, the meaning of the imagery is not obvious, so she must be called on to interpret the message, which allows her to choose to whom and when she talks about her miscarriages. The tattoo, however, gives her an entry point from which to begin the conversation, and in this way, it allows her to discuss loss, remapped and remembered on her body.

Suffering a miscarriage is a loss that is rarely discussed or even shared beyond one's own family,[26] and tattooing this sort of loss on one's arm makes it possible for the event to become sharable. Tattoos are narrative starting points, and people who have them like to share the stories behind them; it is part of what makes tattoos so appealing—they allow one to share one's history. In developed countries where mortality rates are low, such as the United States, the death of a child is one of the more taboo subjects. Several hundred years ago, it was common for a family to lose at least one child to disease or poor hygiene, and there were several socially accepted practices in place for mourning the death of a child. (A drawing or a lithograph or, more recently, death photography of children was quite common; it gave parents a permanent reminder of their dead children.) Now, however, it is rare to experience the death of a child in the United States, and parents who have lost a child find themselves confused and conflicted by a society that not only is uncomfortable with death but avoids speaking about the death of children. Some parents, asked how many children they have, don't know whether to include their dead child among that number, and other parents who have never experienced that loss can be confused by the inclusion of a dead child in a family. Tattoo memorials provide a material and tangible reminder of the child's existence, not only for the parent but for the community as well. Tattoo memorials for deceased children map a landscape of loss on the grieving parent's body.

In the West tattooing a memorial for miscarriage or child death is actually becoming a widespread practice, and there are several websites where parents of deceased infants and children display their tattoo memorials and tell the stories behind the tattoos. These are support chat rooms and grieving sites for such parents. One such site is titled "Infants Remembered in Silence," and there is a special section of this website dedicated exclusively to tattoo memorials.[27] Another is a subsection of a site called The Bump, a pregnancy resource site, but also a site for mothers in general, that is for mothers who have lost their infants (either during pregnancy or after), and community participants are invited to post both photos of their tattoo memorials of their children and the stories behind these memorials.[28] Several of these blog posters write that they were not a "tattoo sort of person" before their loss, but that they wanted something to remind them of their children, accessible at all times and visible to others. The tattoo, then, serves as a permanent and public marker of the mourner's status as bereaved, while also allowing the griever to carry the dead with her in a way that is meaningful and constant. In one dialogue between two mothers who had both lost their children and had procured tattoo memorials following their losses, one told the other that her husband had commented to her that her tattoo "was the only thing that I could actually take to the grave with me, everything else will eventually go away."[29] The two mothers remarked that they liked this idea and found it comforting—that though their children could no longer be with them, their memories of their children, as symbolized by the tattoos they carried, would be with them forever. Reinforcing this idea of a tattoo following one into death, the second mother told the first, "It's the only thing you can physically carry with you no matter where you go and it'll never leave you."[30] This idea of permanence is part of what makes tattoos unique: though they *can* be removed (with large amounts of both pain and money), once they are etched into the skin, they are permanent reminders and part of the enduring landscape of one's body. Tattoos help shape one's identity and reflect one's identity on a public (sometimes private) canvas that cannot be erased except through great effort or death itself. In this way, tattoos are potent symbols of internal constructions of identity.

The fact that these memorials are uploaded to these websites is important; not only are parents getting tattoo memorials for their deceased children, but they are then using them as their emblems for belonging to the community. Taking a picture of the memorial tattoo and displaying it online for others who have experienced loss can be a comforting act that lets grievers understand that they belong. Their memorial tattoos give them access to this world and allow them to bond in ways that they may not have otherwise. They also allow for a positive action that reaffirms the need to grieve and discuss their loss. The narratives shared about the losses are heartbreaking, but they are also community-building, and the parents know that their loss is not unique or solitary.

One of the more common images used in child death memorial tattoos is a child's footprints or handprints. The loss of the child is literally imprinted on the body of its mother or father, and the tattoo is unmistakable in terms of content. It is not only parents, though, who get these memorial tattoos: sometimes it is siblings. One of the more unusual memorial tattoos I have seen belonged to a young college woman in one of my classes. The student was in her late teens, Caucasian, and of no particular religious persuasion (according to her, at least), and taking my World Religions class as a general education requirement for her associate's degree. She had the footprints of her stillborn older brother tattooed on her shoulder. The tattoo clearly was one of a baby's footprints, and when I asked the wearer about it, she told me about her brother. Though this student had never met her brother, she sought out his footprints from her mother as a way to honor his memory on her own body. At first, this seemed strange— a tribute to a sibling who had been born and died before she had been born herself—but perhaps this tattoo said much about this young girl's place in her family—the younger sister of a dead brother. She was born into a family that had already suffered loss and death and did not regard healthy birth and childhood as a given. In short, she forever lived in the shadow of her dead brother, and to commemorate her place in the world and give honor to the deceased brother she had never met, tattooing his footprints on her skin may have been one of the best ways in which to secure her own place in the family. By engraving her brother's footprints on her shoulder, this girl was both brother and sister; she was the keeper of memories she had never experienced herself. Her tattoo was an expression of grief she never personally experienced, but when it was inscribed on her skin, it allowed her to situate herself within her family and community. Tattoo memorials can map our place in the world.

Remembering Grandparents: Tattoos as Bereavement Badges

On the complete opposite end of the spectrum, numerous tattoo memorials are inked in honor of deceased grandparents, and they are often done on people in their twenties. Frequently (but not always) these are the first losses experienced by the tattoo wearer, and the choice to get a tattoo is made as a way of honoring the deceased grandparent. Similarly, young men (and, more rarely, women) who join the military and experience their first deaths in the battlefield are also choosing to commemorate and honor a fallen comrade through a tattoo remembrance (I will discuss this a bit later). The tattoo thus functions as a recognizable rite of passage as much as an emblem for remembrance. Again, like the parents of deceased children, grandchildren and friends are often on the outskirts of the mourning community and frequently do not have a recognized social status as bereaved. Illustrating this is the fact that while workplaces and schools might have policies regarding the death of an immediate family member (almost always a parent or a spouse), there is no place in contemporary society for the friend or even the grandchild. Mourning is often considered the exclusive domain of the immediate family, but it is clear from the popularity of memorials for friends and grandparents, and also by the way in which social network memorials are used by these more marginal communities, that there is a desire or a need not only to be recognized as part of the mourning community, but also to have a space to grieve. Most of these alternative loci of grieving—bodiless memorials, tattoos, car and T-shirt memorials, and Internet memorials—are evidences of mourners, unrecognized by society as such, seeking a place for experiencing the rituals of loss. Mourners traditionally marginalized or left out of grieving are creating new rituals to mourn the dead. Just as spontaneous memorials, emerging at the sites of killings, carve a geographical space in the landscape of the living in order to mourn a loss, tattoo memorials provide a symbolic language through which mourners can share their collective and individual losses. The difference, however, is that people are mapping the space to mourn on their bodies, creating permanent (at least until death) markers of loss on the landscape of the living—indeed, on living bodies themselves. Spaces are often defined by how the living interpret and inscribe themselves on those spaces (e.g., a house and its various rooms, whose functions are defined by people), and tattooing seems to go one step beyond this—by remapping the dead onto bodies in such a way that they are carried around with the living. Memorials for the dead, and sometimes the dead themselves (discussed later in this chapter), are carved onto living bodies.

Many people experience the loss of a grandparent before anyone else close to them dies, and many college-age adults get their first memorial tattoo in honor of a grandparent. Two are discussed here: one consists of the words of a Swedish parenting poem spoken by a grandfather to his children and grandchildren often in his lifetime; it was engraved on the upper part of a foot. The other is a tattoo depiction of a Picasso dove on the upper right shoulder, which reminded the wearer of the copious numbers of birds that flocked to the family's house after her grandmother passed away. Neither of these was a literal representation of the deceased but, rather, a token of the deceased: the first a favorite poem, and the second a reminder, according to the wearer, that the deceased was still somehow present in her life. Both are memorials, but they are focused more on the participation of the deceased in the wearer's life (one during, and one after), than on a preoccupation with death. Though neither of these tattoo memorials *looks* like a memorial, they both are in fact described by the wearers as memorials. When I asked about their tattoos, both wearers told me immediately that theirs were actually not *normal* tat-

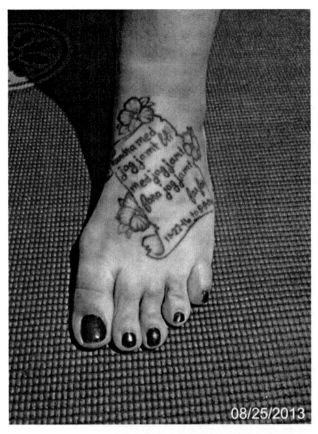

Besides the grandfather's birth and death dates, this memorial tattoo contains a poem that says (in Swedish), "Walk with me always, Guide me always, and Be with me forever, grandfather!" The placement of the tattoo on the foot is intentional, as the wearer said, "I put it on my foot, so he will help me with each step I take." Photo by Brooke Borg

08/25/2013

This tattoo was inked in memory of the wearer's grandmother, who gave her the necklace shortly before she died. Copyright Baylor University; Travis Taylor, *Baylor Lariat*, October 18, 2013, http:// baylorlariat. com/2013/10/18/ from-ashes-to- tats/

toos, but were in remembrance of their grandparents who had died recently, and that these tattoos thus differ significantly from other tattoos because of the meaning behind them. What was interesting to me was the need of the tattoo wearers to assert the uniqueness of their tattoos, emphasizing the fact that the memorial tattoo, because it was a memorial first and tattoo second, was *different* from other tattoos, when, in fact, many young people begin acquiring tattoos through inking a memorial tattoo. Memorial tattoos, while they may look decorative, have an alternative function—they serve as meaning-making symbols that allow the bereaved to feel their identities as mourners, but they also give permission to the tattoo wearers to tell their stories of loss and talk about death in a way that is nonconfrontational. All tattoos have meaning, but they are also meaning-making, creating community between the tattooed and the observer in a way that is fixed and dynamic at the same time.

The Body as Memorial Canvas: Tattoo Placement and Its Importance

Also important to tattoos and their wearers is the physical location of the tattoo itself. The woman with the poem tattoo chose to engrave it on her foot because she said that this meant she would always walk with her grandfather. She felt that engraving the poem on her foot meant that not only were his words always with her, but that he was walking with her in life. She also said that she could look down and see that he was with her; she chose her foot because it would always be visible to her, and she could look down and think about her grandfather at any time. Placement of the tattoo is symbolic and intentional for many wearers. A mother who lost her child chose to tattoo her daughter's hand on her upper thigh because, she said, that was where her daughter would often place her hand when she was learning to walk. Tattooing her daughter's hand was a symbolic imprint of a memory engraved in skin. Another woman wrote, "I plan on getting Avery's foot print on my left foot in the same position as my foot. The left side because he is on the side with my heart, and the foot because he walks with me everywhere, and his foot on my foot because his tiny footprints made a huge imprint on my heart." Again, here the tattoo was to be inked in a very visible part of the body, and not hidden—the tattoo of a foot on her own, an invitation to remember, communally, her son through discussion of the tattoo. Yet another tattooed the name of her deceased child on the skin above her heart, claiming, "i got a tattoo of an angel sitting on a cloud and i got it on my left breast this is so it is over my heart and im always tellin ppl what this tattoo means to me."[31] The placement of tattoos functions as memory maker as much as memory keeper, and it can serve as a reminder of the deceased, giving him or her a new and ongoing place in life on the canvas of someone's skin.

Tattoo memorials are intentional not only in placement on the skin, but in the act of being etched on a canvas that is often visible to others. Tattooing is often done with other people in mind. One young man, Hector Noriega, says that he got his tattoo to help remember his little brother, who died at age twelve from cancer; he feels that having a tattoo will help him remember because people will ask him about it. "I felt kind of like I was forgetting a lot about him," Noriega said. "I felt as though the memories were fading and he wasn't as prominent on my mind, and that upset me. I felt like if I continued the path I was on I would forget about him completely."[32] Noriega got his tattoo so that people would ask him about it, and in being given the audience to share his memories of his brother, he could keep those memories alive. The tattoo was placed with an audience in mind. This echoes Louis Marin's assertion that symbols function as both presentational and representational—symbolic and literal—with a double consciousness of both spectator and wearer.[33] Though art may be inscribed on canvas for an imaginary spectator, tattoos have three audiences in mind: the dead (no longer present), the wearer of the tattoo (whose goal of inscribing the tattoo is to memorialize and, at the same time, function as canvas), and the spectator, expected and sought out. Even those who have acquired tattoos in places that can be concealed have had some sort of spectator in mind, albeit perhaps a more private audience, and the act of concealing is just as revealing (if not more so) of the awareness of the spectator.

While much of the discussion here has linked tattooing to marginalized grieving, it is also a way of marking one's rites of passage in life, as well as securing one's identity both as an individual and in a

This memorial is placed on the side of the torso, where it takes up a large portion of the body. Photo by Dodge (Koi Tattoo)

Another example of a portrait memorial. Photo by Dodge (Koi Tattoo)

A young man received this scorpion tattoo in memory of his father, who was killed by the family's pet scorpion when the boy was seven. The tattoo honors his father's memory with an image of his father's killer, which links father and son through the real and the metaphorical. Copyright Baylor University; Travis Taylor, *Baylor Lariat*, October 18, 2013, http://baylorlariat.com/2013/10/18/from-ashes-to-tats/

group. Military tattoos have long been used (and more widely studied) as male (and now female) bonding rituals between members of a military unit that can help secure identity and also mark significant events. Much has been written about the "collecting" of tattoos by sailors to mark their journeys around the world.[34] These tattoos bond sailors, but they also allow the body to act as canvas, mapping out a journey and preserving memories on skin. Tattoos also serve as a way to remember collective experiences between individuals who will return to their individual lives. Michael May writes that there are four main types of military tattoos, the fourth category being the memorial tattoos of friends who have been killed in action.[35] One of the men May writes about reflects on his memorial tattoo: "You carry a lot of baggage as a soldier," he says. "Losing guys like that. So I just decided to do something external the rest of the world can see."[36] Again, the idea that the tattoo is an externalization of experienced loss, and a public marker of one's identity as mourner, is crucial.

Tattoo Memorials for Survivors of Suicides

Suicide is another death that resides in the margins of society. Suicide for many is a taboo subject that is often covered up or minimally discussed. Like memorial tattoos for deceased infants and children, tattoos to memorialize a death by suicide are becoming common. In fact, just as there are sites for parents of deceased children, there are many Internet websites displaying tattoo memorials remembering the deaths of people who committed suicide; the bereaved upload and display these tattoo memorials. On Facebook, for example, there is a site called The Alliance of Hope for Suicide Survivors, with an album specifically dedicated to pictures of tattoo memorials.[37] The site currently has over 1,400 members, and there are ninety photos of different memorial tattoos. Here again, the ritual of being tattooed (often on the deceased person's birthday or date of death as a way to commemorate materially the place in time) is complemented by photographing and uploading the image of the tattoo, which then places the bereaved firmly and publicly in the community. The tattoo commemorates, but it also unifies, bringing the wearer into a community that understands and shares the loss. Another example of this is a website memorializing a young teenager, Tim, whose parents started the website to help other families and kids dealing with suicide and its effects. On the site's homepage, Tim's parents display their tattoo memorials in a subheading titled "Memorial Stuff" for Tim, telling the story of each tattoo, its placement, and why they received it.[38]

Memorial Tattoos in Asia and Latin America

In Asia, as I discussed earlier, tattoos are traditionally associated with criminals and marginal sectors of society, and these ideas persist today. In China the general public is still relatively wary of tattoos, though celebrity and youth culture and the tattoos associated with them are beginning to popularize tattoos and tattoo culture. There are several tattoo shops in China, and there are even tattoo institutes emerging, teaching tattooing to interested students. As tattoos gain popularity, and national tattoo conventions occur fairly regularly in Beijing, it will not be long before tattoo memorials become a popular form of remembering in China as well. Globalization is not merely for McDonald's and Starbucks; other forms of middle-class status symbols, such as tattoos, are fast becoming prevalent among both the privileged and the well-traveled. China, however, is a bit different from Japan, where a long-standing association of tattoos with Japanese organized crime (*yakuza*) seems to keep tattooing firmly on the fringes of society. In Saitama prefecture (just north of Tokyo), for example, several bills went into effect in 2013 regarding youths under eighteen receiving tattoos, whereas in Osaka, laws are in place that prevent the hire of tattooed individuals for public service jobs.[39] In addition, Saitama pools and water parks do not allow admittance to anyone with a tattoo, and many foreigners report being denied entrance to Japanese *onsen* (hot springs) because they have tattoos.[40] Public opinion regarding tattoos remains mostly negative, and little attention is paid to the symbolism or meaning behind tattoos. For this reason tattoo memorials in Japan are still relatively unpopular, and memorialization does not seem to be a major force behind tattoo acquisition.

Interestingly, tattoos are more popular among Latin American immigrants in the United States than they are in Latin America themselves, and like the car-decal and T-shirt memorials I will discuss in chapter 3, tattoo memorials seem to represent a marginal voice. In the United States that marginal voice rests partly in the immigrant communities that have left their traditional customs behind. As I mentioned earlier, tattoos in Latin America are still considered too expensive by many and are also associated with marginal sectors of society. In fact, in one tattoo shop I visited in Buenos Aires, the shop owner was suspicious of my wanting to interview him. He said that he did not know me, he could not trust me, and did not understand why I would want to research tattoo memorials. My reception in tattoo shops in Mar del Plata, Argentina, was a bit different. Here, as they are in Hawaii, tattoos are a part of an emerging youth culture that has discretionary income and depends on tattoos as a means to define identity. At the Mar del Plata shop Eikel Tattoo, the staff combine tattooing and piercing, whereas at Lucho Tattoo shop in the same town, tattooing is the only service. Memorialization does occur, and the images are somewhat similar to those used in the United

States, though there seems to be a strong preference for inking people's portraits on the body, usually a black-and-white head and shoulders, very lifelike.[41] Essentially, these tattoos are small photographs on the body, permanent remembrances of the dead, inked on a shoulder or on the back (a larger canvas is sometimes needed for these). Here the image of the dead is a representation of the living at his or her most vibrant, the deceased person almost always smiling from the mourner's skin. These photo-tattoos are reminiscent of Catholic Latin American remembrance cards passed around at the memorial Masses in honor of the dead on the anniversaries of their deaths. These cards often have a picture of the deceased, along with birth and death dates and a prayer in honor of the deceased. Operating as keepsakes that can inspire prayer to and for the dead, these photo-tattoos are more permanent images etched into the skin of the bereaved.[42] Again, as in the United States, tattoos as memorials carry a double meaning, which may allow the tattoo to be more socially acceptable than another sort of tattoo would be.

Memorial Tattoo as Process: Cutting the Flesh to Grieve the Body

One of the important elements of tattooing is the process of tattooing itself. Depending on the size and complexity of the tattoo, the process can take anywhere from an hour to several days and repeat visits, and I would posit that the *act* of tattooing is itself a ritual for the mourner. There are aspects about the act of tattooing that are not unlike religious acts, such as the Christian and Hindu mortifications of the flesh, the Buddhist shaving of the hair and eyebrows, the Catholic confessional—and its modern, secular equivalent of seeing a therapist. The act of tattooing is a liminal process in which one is invited to share the meaning behind the tattoo one has chosen, and the tattoo artist is invited to inscribe and translate this meaning onto the flesh in a symbolic memorial that the bereaved will then carry with him or her. The cutting of the flesh with the tattoo needle is cathartic for many, and several of the people who received memorial tattoos spoke to me of the process itself. Though the tattoo may be an unspoken invitation to the public to participate in the memorialization process, the act of tattooing allows one to carve out time and space to grieve in a safe and welcoming place. Both the tattoo artist and the tattoo receiver are forced to confront the meaning of the tattoo as it is being inked into the flesh; several tattoo artists spoke of the person being tattooed as feeling free to speak about the dead, remember the dead, share stories about the dead, and even cry during the process. Where one previously may have felt it was socially unacceptable to cry, the act of cutting the flesh gives one a reason to cry out in pain and to transform one pain into another. In this way the tattoo artist is not unlike a priest or therapist in his or her function, creating a space in which to grieve and a ritual that not only marks the remembrance of the person who died, but also serves as a badge of the process of cutting itself.

The Tattoo Artist as Modern Memorial Maker

I conducted several interviews of tattoo artists in Hawaii on the island of Oahu in the process of writing this chapter.[43] Interviews were informal and were conducted in the tattoo artists' shops, though a formal set of questions began the conversation.[44] All the shop owners noted the prevalent practice of acquiring tattoo memorials, and one artist said that about 20 percent of her shop's work consisted of tattoo memorials.[45] One tattoo artist, Dodge, criticized the popularity of memorial tattoos (as opposed to tattooing as an art form), and noted that the popularity of memorial tattoos may be in part due to the recent popularity of tattoo reality shows, in which tattoos with stories behind them are generally featured. As this artist put it, "Tattoo shows' continual focus tends to be on memorials—to be on the show you have to have a story, so people tend to have tattoos in memorial. Nobody is getting a tattoo for a positive reason."[46] Dodge sees the tattoo as nearly always an emblem of suffering, or of having moved through a difficult stage of life, such as a death or a breakup, or even a birth. Tattoos, in his view, are badges of having moved through these stages and emerged victorious. Another tattoo artist, Shane, pointed toward the physical factors of tattooing as complementing its cathartic aspect, positing: "Tattooing is definitely part of the grieving process. Tattooing releases dopamine in the brain—almost like a stress reliever. It wipes you out after you get tattooed. That's why people keep doing it, too."[47]

Another tattoo artist, Lisa, from Koi Tattoo, emphasized the cathartic nature of the tattooing process itself, stating that people

> get tattoos when they are in pain in their lives. Many women get them when getting divorces; usually people get them when there is a big change in life—cancer, divorce—and the physical pain makes them feel better. [With] drug and alcohol withdrawal, the physical pain helps them get better because it is a physical manifestation of emotional pain. A friend got [tattoos] covered in tiger stripes [and she said that the] "only time I ever get tattooed is when something bad happens and it helps me get through it. The physical pain helps to release the emotional pain." I think it is kind of like how people cut themselves. You are demonstrating a power over the body. A lot of people who get tattoo memorials are still really grieving and in a lot of pain.[48]

When I asked her about the timing for memorial tattoos, Lisa said that most people get them on an anniversary of the death, usually at the one-year point, as a way to mark the death in a meaningful way. She said that many people acquire tattoos as a way to guarantee that they will remember the person, as they feel wearing a memorial will give them a constant visual reminder of the deceased.[49]

As Hawaii is heavily populated by military personnel, all the shops mentioned typical tattoos requested by marines or sailors in memory of their friends. Ash, from Odyssey Tattoo, and Lisa, from Koi Tattoo, said that marines tend to request a gun in a boot, hung with dogtags that are usually inscribed with the names and dates of their fallen comrades. Lisa explained that navy men tend to get anchors with the name and dates of their loved ones. Ash from Odyssey said she tries to discourage people from getting what she believes to be "impersonal" tattoos—common tattoos that other people get to memorialize the dead. She said that most men get skulls or crosses, whereas many women get names, dates, and angels or flowers with which to remember the dead, and she tries to persuade them to choose a tattoo with more personal significance that might directly relate to the deceased. It may also be that the reason for choosing these symbols as part of the memorial tattoo is that they are culturally valued, and they ensure that the tattoos are instantly recognized as memorials; more "personal" tattoos may not be identifiable to others. While Ash agreed with this observation, she was more concerned that perhaps in five or ten years a tattoo might lose its significance and be less valued by the person because of its impersonal character. As Ash put it, "I have a tattoo of a Windex bottle that says, "Put some Windex on it," because that reminds me of my grandma. . . . I try and talk people into getting something more personal because it has more of a connection . . . an inside feeling or joke. . . . I want them to want the tattoo for their whole life and not regret it years down the road."[50] The tattoo artist is contemporary society's shaman or priest—helping

(Above left) A traditional military tattoo that was inked on a soldier who had lost four friends in the war and wanted to make sure he did not forget them; he inked the dogtag initials on his body. Note both the religious and military imagery. Photo by Shane (Eastside Tattoo) *(Above right)* Another example of a military tattoo, in memory of a soldier lost by his friend. Most military tattoos mourn friends and colleagues lost in combat. Photo by Shane (Eastside Tattoo)

Ash, a tattoo artist, favors personal memorials like this one that capture the personality of the person being memorialized in a way that is meaningful to the tattoo wearer. Ash's grandmother used Windex as a fix-all and would tell people to "Put some Windex on it" if something needed to be cleaned or fixed. Ash thought this was the best way to honor her grandmother in a funny yet endearing way. Photo by the author

the bereaved navigate the difficult world of mourning and creating meaningful symbols and rituals that essentially help grievers remember the dead in a meaningful way.

Carrying the Dead with Us: Cremains as Tattoo Memorial

Some tattoo memorials go one step beyond simply remembering the deceased, using the loved one's cremated remains (cremains) as part of the ink in the tattoo. These tattoos are not merely representational memorials, but actually *literal* memorials, with pieces of the dead firmly in place and forever part of the memorial embedded in skin. This practice is so prevalent that there are do-it-yourself videos available online at ehow.com demonstrating the step-by-step process of mixing the cremains with tattoo ink to be ready for etching on skin. One video demonstrates how to make the ink from ashes, and the other shows how to make a tattoo from the ash-infused ink.[51] This may verge somewhat on the morbid, but there are those who find it comforting. The practice of incorporating cremains into the tattoo itself is growing rather than diminishing. The use of the deceased's body is also not entirely new; in the Victorian era it was common to make jewelry out of the hair of the deceased (such as a locket or a brooch) and to wear the jewelry in remembrance of the dead.

Though several of the tattoo artists I interviewed had received requests to ink a tattoo with ashes, only one had actually used cremains as part of the ink.[52] The primary reason was licensing; it is against Hawaii's state health regulations to employ cremains in the ink of a tattoo. That being said, Shane said he had received a request that day, and he would not refuse such a request from someone he knew, as he also thought it might be a cathartic and important process. Dodge, the owner of Koi Tattoo, had received a request from a friend who had lost someone who had been a father figure to him, and he requested that Dodge put the ashes in his skin. Dodge didn't feel as though this practice was as unusual as it sounds, and he pointed to the Japanese practice of burning a hundred-yen bill and putting the ashes of the bill in tattoo ink as a way of ensuring good luck and future wealth. He also discussed the practice of burning black chess pieces and adding the residue to the ink for prison tattoos, so the practice of turning material items into wearable ink is not limited to cremains.[53] The tattoo as text and symbol functions as presentational symbol when the cremains of the dead are inserted into the ink; tattoos are no longer representational inscriptions memorializing the dead, but actually the dead themselves, remapped onto skin, and made into flesh again.[54]

Tattoo Memorials in a World without Grieving

Tattoo memorials are indicative of a deeper societal and cultural need, as they are replacing more traditional forms of mourning that were once familiar and culturally embedded. As little as one hundred years ago, it was common to observe mourning at a person's death; the bereaved would wear mourning clothing, armbands, and memorial jewelry, observing a certain period of socially condoned and expected mourning. Philippe Ariès writes that mourning had a double purpose: "It constrained the family of the deceased to demonstrate, at least for a certain period, a sorrow it did not always feel . . . [and] . . . served to protect the grieving survivor from the excesses of his grief."[55] In other words, the practice of mourning allowed for the recognition of the grieving community as a whole, and it put in place socially recognized customs that benefited both the bereaved and the community in which the bereaved belonged. In Victor Turner's words, the bereaved entered a socially recognized state of *communitas*, and the temporary nature of the bereavement was framed by temporal limits, marked spatially through clothing and the ritual of socially recognized withdrawal from society.[56] Bereavement was a temporary state, but as Ariès so succinctly explains, it had the function of enforcing a ritually observed time of mourning, whether or not the bereaved wanted to observe it. The benefit of this, and what is sorely lacking in today's industrial world, is the socially recognized function of grieving, and the status markers that accompany this function. The loss of a recognized and fixed mourning period is also a loss of the social recognition as a mourner that is necessary for the individual to grieve. As Ariès posits, grief today is supposed to be hidden, private, and secret, and it is no longer publicly sanctioned.[57] In short, the funeral has no separate space in our lives; mourning is no longer a liminal period during which one contemplates the power of life and the finality of death. In contemporary society, particularly in the developed world, mourning is done privately, if at all, and society has no room for the bereavement process: little time is taken off from work for grieving, special clothes are not worn after the funeral itself, and the bereaved are feared or even ostracized. Nearly all the tattoo artists I interviewed were concerned with this difficulty of people to identify as bereaved; they feel that the proliferation of tattoo memorials in modern pop culture might in fact point to an underlying inability of society to recognize the bereaved as mourners. One tattoo artist, Shane, inked a tattoo on a client *before* the death of his friend Lou. In this instance, the tattoo was a way of preparing for Lou's impending death, while also giving the client a symbolic gesture that Lou immediately recognized and treasured. The tattoo was inked with Lou's birth date and a favorite image, in the traditional "Sailor Jerry" style of a pinup girl in a cocktail glass, and it was only *after* Lou's death that the client called Shane requesting that the death date be filled in. In this way, the tattoo artist functions as priest, friend, and counselor in contemporary society, providing an acceptable avenue for mourning, preparing for death, and acting on one's status as bereaved. As Dodge, of Koi Tattoo, expressed:

> In the military, for example, these young kids are told, "Don't leave your buddy behind . . . you guys are brothers. . . . Protect each other." If one of their friends actually gets hurt or dies, they feel like it's their fault, like they messed up or did something wrong, and they are taken out of the field because they are injured, and then they are even more desperate. For these kids, not having seen a whole lot of life, they need pretty strong memorials. The memorials are not for someone they grew up with their whole life. [It's for somebody] they maybe knew for two years. . . . There is an accelerated death rate, and the mortality rate for an eighteen-year-old military grunt is a much higher mortality rate, and they need a tattoo to deal with everything they went through.[58]

Dodge understands the need for people to be recognized as bereaved by society, but his comments (and those of nearly every other tattoo artist I interviewed) illustrate the concern for those who might feel they have no way to express their grief except through memorial tattoos. Freud's concern about "prolonged mourning" or "pathological mourning" can barely be taken seriously in a society where it is not acceptable to mourn, to identify oneself as bereaved, or even to talk about death.[59]

With employment policies now barely giving family (and never friends) time to grieve (or even to organize the disposal of the dead), tattoo memorials serve as public markers on one's body of one's status as bereaved. Though tattoo artists will tattoo a memorial on someone seeking to remember his or her deceased loved one, all the tattoo artists I interviewed expressed an underlying concern about

This tattoo was sought by a client as a memorial to honor his friend Lou, who was going to die soon. Lou has since died, and the client will be adding his death date to the tattoo. Photo by Shane (Eastside Tattoo)

the focus on memorials as tattoo subjects. As Dodge explained, "If I am doing a memorial tattoo, I want it to be a nice tattoo—not this guy died, and it sucked. Once in a while I will do a totally morose, super-sad tattoo. One guy lost his child, and we did a fetus on him. His grief was heavy, so he needed something to release his pain. I wouldn't say yes to doing a tattoo like that on just anybody—but that guy—he needed that and needed something like that to get through his pain."[60] The body serves to illustrate the relationship of the individual to her or his world—governed as it is by empire, state, and society itself. Bodies are subjected to employment, punishment, reproduction, and production, and it is the body's skin that serves as mediator, both literal and figurative, of the body in the world. Skin is stretched, pulled, tightened, tattooed, punished, tortured, and pampered, becoming at once a reflection of social status and identity. De Certeau writes that both the weapon and the tattoo needle organize "social space: it [the tattoo needle] separates the text and the body, but it also links them, by permitting the acts that will make the textual 'fiction' of the model reproduced and realized by the body."[61] In this way, skin is both canvas and map, representation and guide to the world around us, and the tattoo serves as a history of the individual's relationship with the world and with those around him or her. Memorial tattoos, private and public, personal and collective, offer alternative ways to remap the imagination regarding the dead and the ways we remember them.

3

Moving the Dead

The Moving Shrine: Car Memorials and T-Shirt Remembrances

This chapter examines the role of *place* in remembering the dead. Shifting from memorials that one inscribes bodily, we study various other forms of moving shrines, specifically, car memorials and T-shirt remembrances. These nonpermanent memorials function as ways in which people can "carry the dead" with them, without fixing them in place permanently, as tattoos do. The practice of remembering the dead as part of one's identity has its origins in mourning practices such as wearing mourning sackcloth (Hebraic culture) or taking three years off from work and wearing mourning clothes (Chinese culture). And as little as a hundred years ago, in the United States it was common practice for mourners to wear black clothing for a particular period of time (usually for at least a few months, up to a year), and for those not in the immediate family to wear black armbands in solidarity with the grieving.

In the contemporary world, where one is not given much time off from work and society to actually mourn and process a death, or to withdraw from the world, the practice of displaying one's status as mourner becomes even more valuable. This status, however, as it was in traditional mourning practices, is transitional, and thus the car-decal and T-shirt memorials operate as ways of both affirming one's status as a mourner and allowing one to move away from this status once an appropriate amount of time has passed. In this way, these memorials not only allow space and time to reconnect the dead with the living, but also let the bereaved express their memory and mourning in a material and visible way, which is intentionally shared in the public sphere. The pressures on traditional ways of mourning and remembering have caused modern grievers to find new ways in which to remember and grieve, particularly in relation to self-identification. The limits of space and time on mourning, the marginalization of talk of death to a private realm, which is often invisible and undervalued in the public sphere, and the shift from traditional religious expressions of mourning to an individualized and highly commodified transient public expression of mourning have led to some of these contemporary trends: car-decal memorials and T-shirt memorials. Now the dead are no longer merely in their graves; they move with us in the realm of the living.

Decals and Bumper Stickers: Cars as an Extension of Self

Car memorials have become popular within the last twenty years or so, and car-detail shops and vinyl decal companies note that the memorial business has increased both in popularity and in volume within the last decade. Car memorials are usually temporary, removable stick-on decals, often with the name and birth and death dates of the deceased, placed in the rear window of a car in memory of a deceased person. The car becomes a kind of dedication or a loving tribute to the deceased. The car essentially becomes a tombstone. Car-memorial decals often also depict the hobby or favorite activity of the deceased and may include a personal inscription or saying to or about the deceased from the owner of the car. Sometimes religious, but more often not, the saying is a brief tribute such as "Never Forgotten," "Always Remembered," or simply "In Memory of ——." The range of ages of the deceased at the time of death varies widely in these car memorials, though both car-decal manufacturers I spoke with mentioned the high prevalence of memorials for babies and children.[1]

Car decals are personal and indicative of identity, operating in some ways like bumper stickers or refrigerator magnets. Bumper stickers are essentially traveling signposts that reveal one's political leanings, hobbies, and interests to the world around one, personaliz-

Car-decal memorials generally memorialize the deceased much as a tombstone does—with the name, birth and death dates, and sometimes a phrase or nickname familiar to those close to the deceased. Photo by Vinyl Disorder

In Loving Memory

"BoBo"
6/24/84 ~ 5/22/12
Samanta Cox Blanton

ing one's car so that one's own personality becomes imprinted on it.[2] Like social network sites that identify persons as associated with particular politics, hobbies, and friends, bumper stickers allow drivers to identify to the outside world their particular interests and likes or dislikes. Russell Belk examined this idea of people expressing themselves symbolically through their possessions in his examination of the "extended self" and the notion that through our possessions and the ways in which we present them to the outer world, we are making implicit self-statements.[3] Barbara Stern and Michael Solomon refer to the use of bumper stickers in the personalization of cars, writing that "cars are also powerful symbols that express cultural values such as power, freedom, materialism, success, and individualism."[4] In car-dependent cultures such as those of the United States and Australia, cars are essentially an extension of self-identity, conferring status markers such as wealth (or lack of it) and lifestyle through not only the model and make of the car, but its personalization as well. Stern and Solomon summarize this function of cars:

> As expressions of individualism, cars are a canvas for personal
> statements. In addition to the symbolic statement made by the car
> itself, consumers can add self-statements by means of bumper
> stickers and additional symbolic statements by means of other
> ornamentation, such as objects dangling from mirrors, custom
> paint jobs, and elaborate stereo equipment. Bumper stickers
> represent a unique ornamentation category in that they convey
> direct consumer statements—self-proclamations, names of kinship

groups, messages about the self or directives to others, epithets, boasts, and so forth—in words. As such, they afford the opportunity to study consumer communication about the self (personal identity) and about the self in relation to others (social identity) in terms of verbal artifacts that the consumer has chosen.[5]

Cars thus function as symbolic extensions of self, and as such, bumper stickers (and other forms of car personalization) offer an additional popular narrative that contributes to cultural discourse. In fact, social psychologists have found that the more personalized a car is, the more a person is actually attached to that car as an extension of self and views the car as a symbol of self-identity.[6] Car-decal memorials are, in short, moving (both literal and figurative) narratives of grief expressed in a personal way. They do this by operating as extensions of the grieving self and using an already existing and accepted form of social discourse: decals and stickers.

Wearing Your Heart on Your Bumper: Car Memorials as Moving Remembrances

The MADD bumper sticker, which emerged in the early to mid-1980s, is probably the earliest precursor to the modern-day car-decal memorial. This sticker was sponsored by Mothers Against Drunk Drivers, whose children had been killed in automobile accidents caused by drunk drivers. The mothers placed the bumper stickers on their cars both as a way of identifying themselves as mothers who had lost children, and as a tool for social protest. It was very effective on both counts, and drivers and the American Congress paid attention, as more punitive laws were enacted against drunk drivers, and drunk driving became more socially unacceptable. Eventually, however, other drivers began to express solidarity by also affixing MADD stickers to their bumpers, and these bumper stickers were no longer a form of self-identification of personal loss. They became an indication of agreement with the cause against drunk driving. Once stricter legislation was passed in Congress, the prevalence of MADD stickers decreased, and now these stickers are rarely seen and almost never associated with personal loss.[7]

The first car-decal memorial that emerged on a popular level for an individual is believed to be one in memory of the NASCAR driver Dale Earnhardt Sr., who died in the Daytona 500 race in February 2001. Following his death, many drivers, particularly in the South, placed memorial decals in their rear windows with Earnhardt's car number, 3, sometimes accompanied by angel's wings, and the words "In memory of Dale Earnhardt" or simply "In Memory of." In September of that year, following the attack on the World Trade Center, many people began to affix both bumper stickers and car-decal memorials to their cars with the words "We will not forget" and the American flag.[8] Both of these examples, like the MADD bumper stickers, demonstrated mass popular responses using cars as canvases. Earnhardt's memorial decals, though, most closely resemble car-decal memorials as they are seen today. The standard template is nearly the same: birth and death dates, the name, and a symbolic gesture recognizing the deceased individual's interests and hobbies.

Interestingly, memorialization through car decals has not been widely observed in other cultures, with the exception of Israel, where bumper stickers are used to demonstrate political solidarity and identity. In Israel, immediately following Rabin's assassination in 1995, many cars began sporting bumper stickers with the message "Shalom, Chaver," or "Goodbye, Friend," in honor of the slain statesman. It was at once an outpouring of public sympathy and a display of popular solidarity surrounding Rabin's death.[9] Personalized use of car-decal memorials does not seem to have taken off in Israel as it has in the United States, however, and it seems the majority of car-decal memorials (at least for individuals, rather than political figures) are found in the United States. The reason for this is relatively simple: the United States is a car-dependent culture, and most families own at least one if not two cars. Since cars are seen as an extension of the self, rather than simply a mode of transportation, which they often are in other countries, it is not surprising that car-decal memorials remain relatively scarce in other countries.

Car-Decal Memorials as an Expression of Personal Grief

Car decal memorials are not as mainstream as tattoos. They are, however, cheaper and less permanent. Unlike tattoos, which cost

anywhere from several hundred to several thousand dollars, depending on the number of sessions needed to ink, car-decal memorials
cost five to fifteen dollars. Memorial decals are meant to be temporary, generally lasting several years. In fact, it is becoming more and
more common to draw one's own temporary memorial in shoe polish
on one's car, either in lieu of, or in addition to, affixing a traditional
memorial decal. Almost immediately following the death of the deceased, grievers will draw a memorial on the rear and side car windows in shoe polish, writing a poignant message in memory of the
deceased, such as "We will miss you, ——" or "RIP ——." Sometimes these messages are written on cars while the mourners gather
to attend the funeral or memorial service and then are later replaced
by car-decal memorials. At other times these temporary memorials
are the only moving memorials, left until the next rain washes them
away. The impermanent aspect of the car memorial is reinforced by
the fact that the owner of the car is *in* the car for only a limited
amount of time, and the driver is identified with the car memorial
only as long as he or she is driving or sitting in the car. Once the
driver returns to work or home, however, he or she is no longer personally affiliated with the messages on the car, and in this way the
memorial functions more like clothes than a tattoo. Additionally,
car-decal memorials as a medium are a quick and easy way to let others know about one's grieving status, particularly in an era in which
time is important and driving is almost universal. Like virtual memorials on social networks, car-decal memorials are fast becoming rec-

A newly emerging
practice seems to be the
short-term shoe-polish
memorial—declaring to
the world one's new
status as bereaved
through one's car. As cars
have become extensions
of identity and class, it is
no surprise that they also
function as sites of grief.
Photo by the author

ognized in American car culture as a readily identifiable symbol of grief and mourning. In my interviews I have found that people are generally baffled by their emerging popularity and unsure of the etiquette surrounding their use.[10]

Car-decal memorials are particularly prevalent in the American borderlands, such as California and Texas, and they may be a commentary not only on the mobile shrines but on the importance placed on American car culture itself. As Nicholas Christenfeld notes, "Cars are now just mobile living rooms, family rooms, kitchens . . . and the symbols of mourning that one might have confined to one's house can now be displayed on one's car."[11] A 2005 *New York Times* article elaborates: "For years drivers in Southern California have been using their cars as whizzing classified ads, announcing everything from house cleaning to property for sale to weight-loss plans. But these days car owners are increasingly using their vehicles as rolling tombstones."[12] Are these car-decal memorials really "rolling tombstones" or, like the MADD bumper stickers, ways of identifying oneself and one's status as bereaved in a meaningful and publicly recognizable way?

Car-decal memorials are much cheaper than other forms of memorialization, and like tattoos, they use a canvas already part of the everyday fabric of a person's life. These memorials function much like Internet memorials in that they are instantly and readily familiar, using a social medium (the bumper sticker) that has a proven track record as an effective way to communicate opinion and identity. Just as users of social networks post pictures of themselves with the deceased as their profile photos to identify themselves publicly as bereaved, garnering social capital within an existing social network, car memorials also function as easily recognizable and visible explanations of a person's status as a mourner. The driver is declaring her or his status as bereaved to both known and unknown people, and she or he is doing it in a way that is a familiar and acceptable form of social discourse. The message is quick and efficient; in a culture dominated by fast-food and drive-through restaurants, texting, and emoticons, car-decal memorials relay a message of grief in a rapid and recognized medium.

In a time when grieving for longer than two weeks for a loved one is classified as a form of depression in the American Psychological Association's *DSM 5* and few workplaces allow more than a few days of absence to grieve over the loss of a family member (and rarely any time for the loss of a friend), the need to mark one's changed status in a public yet transitory way empowers the griever and helps her or him to cope. By acknowledging one's status as bereaved and advertising it through a car decal, one is using one of the few windows (pun intended) available to proclaim one's liminal state to the world. MADD mothers were able to garner sympathy, support, and social change in response to their memorial stickers; perhaps car-decal memorials will allow death to reenter the public arena so that bereavement is not something avoided, but validated and affirmed. Whereas earlier the bumper sticker on the car of a MADD mother seemed somehow appropriate (her child was killed by a car, and that loss was, ironically, being mourned and remembered on a car), however, now the car-decal memorial seems less like an ironic remembrance and more like an additional public space in which to advertise one's status as mourner. The car, then, becomes not only a mobile tombstone, but also a moving shrine—a memorial at once private and public, intentional and self-aware, in announcing to the world the bereavement of the driver.

Car-Decal Memorial Manufacturers: An Accidental Business

I conducted interviews with several of the larger car decal companies, and the most striking similarity among them all is that they intentionally started as manufacturers not of car-decal memorials, but of vinyl decals and signs. It is only through personal requests and a consumer-driven market that the car-decal-memorial business has emerged, and companies have responded to this popular demand by moving some of their decal offerings into the memorial market, doing so with tremendous if unintentional success. These companies range from full-scale national companies with a marked Internet presence to local mom-and-pop decal shops that specialize in anything from signage to car customization and detailing.

One of the largest car decal manufacturers in the United States, Custom Signs Decal Junky (www.decaljunky.com), states that 20 to 30 percent of their decal business consists of memorial decals. They receive orders regularly, not just for individual car-decal memorials, but also for memorials produced in bulk.[13] Many times grieving communities pass out the memorial decals at funerals or memorial services, and they place these memorial decals on their cars in solidarity.[14] According to my interviews, the majority of bulk orders for car-decal memorials honor younger drivers—usually teenagers—who were killed in automobile accidents. These memorials, like the MADD stickers before them, are intended to serve as both memorial and warning. Striving to find a way to make meaning out of an early and traumatic death, the car-decal memorial allows the grieving community to make the deceased person's death meaningful by—it is hoped—helping prevent other deaths in similar circumstances.

Another car decal manufacturer, Vinyl Disorder, has orders for a minimum of one thousand memorial decals a month, and sales are growing exponentially. The majority of these are single-order decals, though occasionally orders come in for twenty-five, fifty, or one hundred, to be handed out at memorial services. The fact that so many of these are individual orders (as opposed to bulk orders) speaks to the huge trend in customization and personalization in grieving death today. In my interviews with Vinyl Disorder, the company said that its client base is largely in the United States, though occasional orders come from Australia. Both the United States and Australia are large car cultures, and, with the exception of larger metropolitan areas, they often lack effective public transportation, so it makes sense that car-decal memorials are emerging in cultures heavily dependent on private transportation. I also asked Vinyl Disorder if, when the company started, it saw car-decal memorials as a large part of its future business, and it said it had not, but these decals have become a large percentage of total sales, so the company has modified its website to offer customers a variety of designs and examples of memorial offerings. There are currently over seven thousand images and designs offered on the site, but the Vinyl Disorder team states that the most popular ones are custom designs that they develop with the customer. Their top-selling and most popular memorial decals are designs with the deceased person's name, dates, and an image of mountains, butterflies, an angel, or angel's wings. Custom work might include a child's handprints or footprints along with the child's name and

In Loving Memory

Robert Loveless

2/11/1993 ~ 10/6/2010

~Just Breathe Now~

Car decals can be mass produced or ordered individually. Their primary function seems to be, like that of tattoos, to announce one's status as bereaved. Photo by Vinyl Disorder

dates, or a picture of an item associated with the deceased's hobby (such as a golf club or a tennis racket); it might even reveal the cause of death.[15]

Like tattoo designs, the design of a car-decal memorial is usually formulaic, containing the name of the person, birth and death dates, a symbol representing the deceased, and often a message from the bereaved to the deceased. These four aspects mark the traditional ingredients of the car-decal memorial. What is notable here is the visual symbol that stands in for the deceased—for babies and children it is often footprints or an angel, and for an older person it is often an image that represents a particular hobby. The body of the deceased is thus replaced by a symbol, whether by footprints ("I was here on this earth"), angel's wings ("I am still here though you cannot see me"), or a golf club ("my father died; he liked to golf"). The symbols given for older people are in some ways more personal and allow observers an entrée into the mourning experience. Car-decal memorials are also highly gendered, as particular colors or symbols are used for each sex, which is perhaps a continuation of the trend in car-decal memorialization to personalize as much as possible the memorial. Last is the message from the bereaved to the deceased. This message is written in both the second person ("You will always be missed") and the third person ("He will always be missed") but generally expresses the grief of the car owner for the deceased. It is almost always highly personal and functions to include the car owner in the grief process. The purpose of the message is to establish the role of the car owner as bereaved. Its function, in many ways, is similar to those of obituaries (to establish who is bereaved) and the current practice of posting a picture with the deceased on one's social network site to advertise one's position in the world as bereaved (which I discuss in more detail in the next chapter). Thus, the car-decal memorial simultaneously serves to remember the dead and establish the car owner's role as bereaved. This personalization of death into a transactional symbol that is an individualized and highly commodified transient public expression of mourning is one of the attractions of car-decal memorials. Consumers can personalize their own memorials, selecting artwork that is meaningful to them and yet remains digestible as a public narrative of mourning.

The impermanence of car-decal memorials, unlike tattoos, is part of their appeal. In a way, these decals can mirror the stages of grieving, and several newspaper articles have highlighted the experience of the griever in moving through the grieving process and watching the decal age and fade or removing the decal altogether once the griever feels there is no longer a need to identify himself or herself as bereaved. In this way, car-decal memorials can function as a new mourning ritual—both in the application of the decal in adopting an identity as a mourner, and in the removal of the decal as the symbol of the griever's readiness (however tentative) to reenter everyday society. This is similar to the traditional function of mourning clothing, whereby one conveyed one's mourning status for a particular period of time, and then reentered society, once again adopting everyday wear. The pain, both cathartic and ritualistic, of removing a car-decal memorial is described in an article in the *Anniston Star:*

> After five years, the decal Daniel Shaw bought for his daughter, Amanda, started to fade and peel. Amanda was six weeks old when she died of heart complications. It was a spontaneous decision when Shaw bought the decal from an online graphics shop. . . .
> But time took its toll. It took Shaw ages to muster the courage to remove the decal.

"I never expected to get so attached," he said, sobbing lightly.
"But taking that thing off, in a small way, was like having to say
goodbye all over again. It hurt, but it also helped me let go.
There's still a spot on my back windshield that's in the shape of an
angel. So she's not really gone."[16]

This ritual, so poignantly recounted here, captures the significance
attached to the car-decal memorial; indeed, it is not merely the sticker itself that is important, but rather, the *process* of applying and then
taking off the decal that the car decal memorial takes on greater
meaning. Applying the car-decal memorial allows Shaw to begin going through the stages of grief in a way that is publicly recognized,
and then, when he is ready, he can emerge from mourning with the
symbolic act of removing the memorial. In this way the car-decal
memorial, and the rituals associated with it, becomes a replacement
for (and sometimes an addition to) religious rituals. It is interesting to
note here that the process of applying the car-decal memorials, like
the inking of tattoo memorials, is an important part of the ritual of
remembering the dead. It is not merely the message conveyed in the
car decal, but also the acts of applying it and peeling it off that become outward symbols of wearing and taking off one's grief.[17]

Sanctification of the Mundane: Cars as Mobile Shrines

When it has a car-decal memorial affixed to it, a car in some ways
operates as a mobile shrine. The memorial is a literal reminder of the
deceased, one that is both consciously and conspicuously used as a
way in which to honor the dead. One life insurance salesman noted
that car decals are often used by people who are left smaller inheri-
tances, which are then used to purchase vehicles, or the car itself is
the inheritance. In this way, the car is "dedicated" to the memory of
the deceased who left behind enough money for the purchase of a
vehicle (but not enough to buy land or a house).[18] When the driver
dedicates the car to the memory of the deceased, the car takes on a
dual function: as transportation and as a moving shrine to honor and
remember the dead. Additionally, this shrine is both portable and
inhabitable, which allows the driver easily to honor the dead without

actually visiting the site of the deceased's remains. Finally, as cars are considered durable goods, recognizing the passing down of such property from the deceased to the bereaved through a car memorial decal is a public (and culturally recognized) way of demonstrating gratitude for both the deceased and the property passed down. Romeo Corpuz, of Pearl City, Hawaii, has a memorial sticker on his car honoring his cousin who died of cancer, from whom he inherited his 1987 silver Honda. Corpuz can remember and memorialize his cousin as he drives his car.[19] In other words, in this instance, it might not merely be a way of remembering the dead, but also a way for the living to affirm their relationships and "special status" with the deceased. With its car-decal memorial, the car is no longer merely an object; it becomes a mobile shrine—a religious artifact inserted into everyday life.

Whose Cars?

One noticeable trend of car-decal memorials is that they tend to be popular among marginal immigrant communities in the United States—in the mainland United States car-decal memorials are widely popular among Latino and Filipino communities. In Hawaii car-decal memorials are found mostly among Filipino, Samoan, and Hawaiian communities, which are minority groups in relation to the larger ethnic enclaves of Japanese, Caucasian, and Chinese people living in the islands. Car decals are not nearly as popular (if evident at all) in South America or in the Philippines themselves, however. In fact, interviews I conducted in both Argentina and Colombia revealed that most people did not even know what car memorials were, and they found the concept a bit strange.[20] Car-decal memorials do exist on a much lesser scale in the United Kingdom, Canada, and Australia. The main reason for this is that car-decal memorials are popular in car cultures, such as the United States, where the landscape is broad and families generally depend on personal transportation to go to and from work and conduct their business. Though there may be the odd car-decal memorial here or there in other areas, in general car-decal memorialization exists in places where (1) the car serves as an extension of self and public identity, (2) the car serves as one of the more readily available methods for personal expressions of grief and remembrance.

Additionally, in my interviews with car-decal manufacturers, all of them noted the fact that there was *no* dominant ethnicity or language; they all also noted the high prevalence of orders for memorials honoring babies and children. In other words, though at first glance car-decal memorials may seem representative of certain ethnicities and their traditions of mourning, they are actually expression of grief for those who are marginalized, whether because they are ethnic minorities within a larger dominant culture or because they have experienced the death of a child and cannot talk about that loss in a culture uncomfortable with children's deaths. Car-decal memorials, like tattoos, are marginal expressions of mourning, and personalization of cars is *more* likely to occur because cars can be, after a house, the most expensive durable good one owns. Thus, like tattoos and Internet memorials, which tend to represent marginal grieving, car-decal memorials represent not only marginal grieving, but grieving in the margins—bereavement by marginal communities outside the dominant American discourse. More material than the Internet, and yet less permanent and durable than the tattoo, car-decal memorials offer a way to express one's mourning in a way that builds on an already established form of popular expression, the bumper sticker.

Mobile Memorials: Mourning the Dead through Clothing

Mourning clothing has long been a primary form of public identification for the bereaved, a recognized way of both proclaiming and claiming one's status as mourner. T-shirt memorials are a very recent update and variation of this traditional expression of remembering the dead. T-shirt memorials are most often T-shirts with digital photo representations of the dead, including the birth and death dates of the deceased, silk-screened in a personalized design, which are handed out at the funeral. Like car memorials, this custom was initially practiced among more marginal communities, particularly Roman Catholic communities in the United States (this is a common practice, for example in the Samoan enclaves in Los Angeles and in Hawaii),

Saint Mary MacKillop

"Never see a need without doing something about it."
Mother Mary MacKillop

Catholic memorial cards allow the dead to be reinserted into the realm of the living through a publicly and religiously sanctioned form of honoring and remembering them. Photo by the author

where the distribution of memorial cards at funerals was already widespread. Catholic memorial cards display a small photo of the deceased and often contain a brief narrative outlining key events of the deceased person's life, along with birth and death dates, and a moving message from the family and friends. T-shirts operate similarly, allowing community members to display their solidarity as grievers, simultaneously giving them something to take home and wear again. Additionally, T-shirt costs in bulk are not much more than the expense of the Catholic remembrance cards, and T-shirt memorials tend to be more popular among younger generations because they can be worn again, and they offer an easy way to memorialize the dead. Now, however, T-shirt memorials extend beyond Catholic communities and are found in all sorts of groups—particularly for those who have died at a young age.

Slate places the origins of T-shirt memorials in West Coast gang culture in the 1990s, but this practice has been around in some way since the emergence of the T-shirt in American fashion in the 1950s, when the iconic white T-shirt became prominent as a mode of self-expression.[21] Memorials honoring dead pop culture figures (Bob Marley, Marilyn Monroe, John Lennon, Che Guevara, for example) have been around much longer than the practice of putting dead gang members on T-shirts. Thus, honoring the dead through T-shirts is not a new phenomenon; what *is* new is the appropriation of popular culture and its traditions to memorialize the local dead. Memorial T-shirts are often manufactured, sold, and worn to commemorate the deaths of famous people. T-shirts for more popular or well-known figures, such as Steve Jobs[22] and Whitney Houston,[23] are sold online on Etsy and eBay. For example, many of Houston's fans wore memorial T-shirts as her funeral procession traveled to the church. The T-shirt as the quintessential "blank slate" of clothing allows one to shape, fashion, and use the T-shirt in much the same way that bumper stickers are used for cars—as an extension of oneself and one's identity—though T-shirts are even more transitory and interchangeable than bumper stickers.

T-Shirt Memorials as Contemporary Mourning Clothing

In many ways, the T-shirt memorial is a modern version of traditional mourning clothing. As I mentioned earlier, it was customary in most societies around the world to wear mourning clothing for a prescribed period to denote one's status as bereaved and to separate oneself from society. Dressing differently allowed both griever and those around him or her the space in which to mourn, and it served visibly to declare the mourner's state as bereaved. After the prescribed period (which ranged from several months to years), the griever would resume wearing his normal clothes and be expected to assume the full functions of normal society. Toward the middle of the last century, this custom was replaced (in many parts of the world, and especially in the United States) with token symbols of mourning, as traditional grieving clothing was reduced to an armband worn for a shorter time. Black armbands allowed the griever to demonstrate his or her status as bereaved while wearing clothing appropriate for work or other duties in society. The armband was removable and yet universally recognizable as a symbol of mourning without being disruptive. Eventually, even armbands were no longer worn, and in today's society there is generally no standard mourning dress for the be-

reaved. Though formal clothing is often worn today to a funeral service, mourning clothing comes in literally all shapes and colors, and
there is no prescribed etiquette customarily observed in funeral dress.
In contemporary America today, for example, the favorite color of
the deceased is sometimes worn to the funeral, rather than the uniform black that has traditionally been worn at funeral and memorial
services. In short, mourning clothing, and the traditions that accompanied it, is no longer part of the funeral ritual and remembrance.

In a society where formal mourning clothes are no longer worn,
and grievers have no set dress code that indicates their status as
mourners, T-shirt memorials allow this status to be claimed in an instantly recognizable way. Memorial T-shirts function like mourning
wear, immediately recognizable as bereavement clothing, yet casual
enough to be worn every day. Like car-decal memorials, T-shirt memorials grant social capital to their wearers, and they can be taken
off in situations in which death is not an acceptable topic of conversation. When they are worn, however, they have the ability to act as
conversation pieces, which is one of the essential functions of the memorial T-shirt—to allow death to enter the conversation. T-shirts are
not formal wear, and they are generally not worn in work environments, so they are usually worn when the wearer is not working or is
sporting casual wear. The conversation that a T-shirt sparks, then, is
one that takes place in a more casual environment and, as is the case
with car-decal memorials, is both desired and intentional.

T-shirt memorials have become so common that there are several
websites for designing and ordering them.[24] Kyle, an agent at CustomInk, one of the larger custom-order T-shirt manufacturing companies, noted that in his three years of employment at CustomInk,
the company has received orders for memorial T-shirts nearly every
day.[25] When asked what the particular demographic was for these
shirts and what kind of images were generally used, Kyle replied,
"The persons being honored on the shirts range from infants to the
elderly. The ones honoring kids tend to be hard to create with the customer without getting teary-eyed. If they don't have an idea of what
they want, I usually go with something heavenly or childlike. Cherubs, kids, a park scene. . . . I try to get a sense of what they liked, favorite color, car enthusiast, profession, et cetera, and then incorporate

that into a design or use items to design into or around their photo."[26] Like tattoo artists, memorial T-shirt designers guide their customers toward more personalization, encouraging designs that reflect the deceased person's own interests, hobbies, and so on. In this way the T-shirt is a personal memorial, much like the tattoo memorials discussed in chapter 2, not just a standard remembrance. The thought and planning involved in creating the T-shirt memorial allow the shirt's wearer to participate in the way in which the dead will be remembered—by choosing a favorite photo of the deceased or a particular phrase about the deceased, along with certain symbols that may represent her or him. It is interesting to note, though, that, as in obituaries, which are often artificially constructed narratives about the deceased, the remembrance is selective and may reveal as much about the person who orders the T-shirts as it does about the deceased.

T-shirt memorials, like car-decal memorials, are inexpensive ways of remembering the dead. As one article points out, "At $10 to $15 per shirt, or around $3.50 if ordered in bulk, they're less expen-

T-shirts like this one could be considered new forms of mourning dress, though they can be deeply personal and somewhat shocking, as the person being mourned is depicted in full color and almost seems alive on the T-shirt. T-shirt and photo courtesy of Mona T-shirt, Houston.

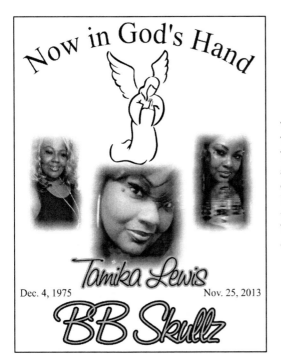

Now in God's Hand

Tamika Lewis

Dec. 4, 1975   Nov. 25, 2013

BB Skullz

Though these memorial T-shirts are all for women, T-shirts memorialize men and women, young and old, though they seem to be more popular among the younger generation. T-shirt and photo courtesy of Mona T-shirt, Houston.

Another example of the mourning T-shirt—contemporary society's new form of mourning dress. T-shirt and photo courtesy of Mona T-shirt, Houston.

In Loving Memory of

Sunrise   Sunset

M   D
a   e
y   c

1   1
9   8

1   2
9   0
7   0
7   8

Cynthia Chivara

La Chinguis

sive than a bouquet of lilies or many teddy bears, which may explain their appeal to teens,"²⁷ but T-shirt memorials can often serve a secondary purpose of raising money for memorial funds honoring the dead. In this way T-shirts provide tangible memorials to the dead but also aid the living—whether through fund-raising efforts to cover the costs of the funeral, or by providing funds for research or raising money for scholarships. Additionally, T-shirts as "take-away memorials" offer a way of extending the space (and time) of grieving into the everyday world. Commemorating the anniversary of the deceased by wearing the T-shirt again allows grievers to form their own rituals that honor the dead, and that also allow for the self-identification of the bereaved. Finally, T-shirt memorials are universally affordable as portable shrines, and the fact that they eventually wear out after repeated wearings and washings emphasizes their temporary nature. They are, in the truest sense, contemporary mourning clothing.

Like car-decal memorials, T-shirt memorials surged in popularity with the events of September 11, 2001:

> Sept. 11 was the "tipping point" that pushed memorial T-shirts into mainstream visual vernacular. In New York and Washington, D.C., people began wearing T-shirts memorializing slain friends, family members, police officers, and firefighters. In many ways, these standard memorial tees resembled the posters that were placed around New York City when friends and families were still searching for their loved ones. In the aftermath of 9/11, many people bought T-shirts featuring the popular "crying eagle," the New York Fire Department logo, or the American flag, turning a once-ironic act into a demonstration of solidarity and mourning. (In 1968, when Abby Hoffman transformed an American flag into a shirt, he was arrested and tried for desecration. Today the Stars and Stripes are slapped onto everything from men's boxer shorts to women's string bikinis.) During the war in Iraq, the flag tee-as-memorial was adopted by the families of slain soldiers. When Army Spc. Larry K. Brown was killed in Iraq last April, his family (including his mother and father) wore T-shirts depicting Old Glory to the funeral.²⁸

T-shirts are mainstream, affordable, and recognizable, and people use them to convey political messages and project a self-image with messages that range from the profound to the silly. For example, "I'm Republican," "Save the Environment," "I'm with Stupid" all send different messages but give observers an insight into deeper aspects of the T-shirt wearer's character, from political viewpoints to sense of humor or lack thereof. It is understandable, then, that one might use the T-shirt as a canvas for mourning, particularly since clothing is one of the most immediate markers of grief that has been used by cultures around the world to demonstrate a person's status as bereaved.

Wearing Your Message: Personal Memorializing in a Public Realm

Like bumper stickers on cars, T-shirts function as a signpost of the wearer's identity and proclaim the wearer's likes and dislikes to the world. They are made with an audience in mind and are worn to be seen, not hidden. Bumper stickers and T-shirts can be seen as personal messages that are to be read in public. John Newhagen and Michael Ancell state that both bumper stickers and T-shirts "allow for the expression of highly personal opinions about strongly held views to a large audience without any real commitment to interact with them."[29] Memorial T-shirts are made expressly for an audience, but for the wearer's benefit, as the message of the T-shirt may, in fact, make others uncomfortable. The wearer of the T-shirt seeks to convey the message that she or he is in mourning and does so quickly and effectively with a memorial T-shirt, which is similar to a car-decal memorial. Memorial T-shirts are the wearers' way of both honoring the deceased and letting the world around them know about their loss: it is a profound message using an everyday medium. Like online chat rooms offering grief support groups and profile pictures with the deceased, memorial T-shirts and car-decal memorials offer a way for wearers to advertise their status as bereaved in an effortless and meaningful way, one that requires little communication beyond the symbolic. Like car-decal memorials, T-shirts are also sometimes distributed at funerals as a way for the grieving community to identify themselves in solidarity with one another in their grieving status. In certain communities across the United States, the T-shirt is a common way to express one's identification with a particular mourning group. As Chino Mizrachi, the owner of a Miami T-shirt shop that specializes in memorial T-shirts, remarked, bereaved customers "know the best place to be together to talk about the guy is the T-shirt place. . . . They have no place else right after. Two, three days after, there's the wake, but when it happens, it's fresh, they all come to me here."[30] Often an immediate family member will take a picture of the deceased to be memorialized on a T-shirt, and a T-shirt shop such as Mizrachi's will keep the picture on file, and soon there will be more orders to be filled for memorial T-shirts. T-shirt memorials function as a starting point for the communal sharing of grief, and they do so in a readily identifiable way. The shirts are then worn to wakes, funerals, and memorial services, and on death anniversaries, the birthdays of the deceased, and simply when the mourner misses the dead. One example is Tiffanie Jones, who has T-shirts for all her friends and family members who have died.

> All told, Ms. Jones, 22 years old, has shirts for eight friends and
> family members murdered in and around her east New Orleans
> neighborhood. She has 10 more shirts for her brother Neal, who
> crashed on his motorcycle, and two shirts for her mother, Mary,
> who died of cancer. Ms. Jones wears one every few days. Or she'll
> just wear a T-shirt around the one-story brick house she shares
> with her grandmother. Family and friends who drop by bring the
> shirts to life. "They'll say, 'You remember when Neal did this? Or
> Rabbit did this?'" Ms. Jones says.[31]

The T-shirt memorial operates much like the car-decal memorial, in that its purpose is intentional: it has an audience in mind, and it is displayed with the desire to allow death to come into everyday discourse. Tiffanie Jones lost ten people in a relatively short amount of time—one from natural causes, and all the others from violence—and chooses to wear memorial T-shirts to demonstrate her losses, but also as a therapeutic way of coming to terms with death. By wearing the shirts, she feels she is able to initiate conversations about her dead mother, brother, and friends, and to demonstrate a desire to discuss the many deaths she has experienced. The wearing of the memorial T-shirt is intentional—not only to mark her status as bereaved, but also to express a desire to discuss the dead, who are no longer part of her life.

One negative aspect of this community-building, though, has been that because it has become a widely accepted form of communal grieving, some feel that it has also become a form of glorifying and celebrating death. In fact, some school principals have found the T-shirt memorials to have a negative effect; far from seeing the T-shirts as a negative reminder of the fragility of life, they believe T-shirt memorials glorify dying young. Dan Morse quotes Ron Taylor, principal of Booker T. Washington Middle and High School in New Orleans, who has banned T-shirt memorials in his schools:

> "Kids see these T-shirts," says Mr. Taylor, who grew up in a New Orleans housing project, "and they say, 'I want to be a thug. I want to die a thug. I want to go out in a blaze of glory.'"[32]

The T-shirts themselves do not glorify death, but in a world without recognized venues for grieving and rituals that are communally accepted and valued, how else can these seemingly meaningless deaths be discussed, understood, and mourned? Kate Moser quotes Jack Santino, a professor of pop culture: "In dealing with death, Americans today often feel they lack the sense of community their grandparents had, says Jack Santino, . . . professor at Bowling Green and editor of 'Spontaneous Shrines and the Public Memorialization of Death.' 'It's almost as if it's a substitute for a close-knit community,' he says. 'You don't really know all these people, but that's the best you can do.'"[33] The need for recognition as a mourner through transactional symbols such as bumper stickers or clothing is not new; what is new, though, is the media of the memorial car decal and the memorial T-shirt—everyday artifacts of contemporary American life—instantly recognizable and simultaneously ubiquitous. Turning these quintessential items of consumer culture into instruments of bereavement forces others to acknowledge death and participate in a dialogue of grief and bereavement. In a world that places limits on space and time for mourning and marginalizes talk about death to the private realm, the shifts from traditional religious expressions in mourning to an individualized and highly commodified transient public expression of mourning seem almost natural and even necessary. Both car-decal memorials and T-shirt memorials allow grievers to declare to the community around them that they are mourning, using aspects of daily life (cars, clothing) to advertise their status as bereaved. Using widely recognized media (bumper stickers, clothing) in new and innovative ways to create highly personalized and recognizable displays of mourning, they are attempting to move their grief out of the margins and into the everyday world, reinserting both death and the dead into the realm of the living.

4

Speaking to the Dead

Social Network Sites and Public Grieving

Packaging the Dead: The Need for Virtual Memorials

Virtual bereavement allows for marginal discourse to circumvent traditional modes of bereavement by reclaiming mourning and the ways we talk and think about the dead. The virtual realm returns us to our mourning through memorialization: through image and memory, without the messiness of the corpse. The language of grief presented in these Internet memorials is popular and spontaneous, but it reflects marginal discourse. The use of written narratives to construct meaning for the dead in the realm of those in mourning is nothing new: both obituaries and elegies have long been a part of the world of mourning. I would argue that this narrative impulse—to construct meaning and a neat chronological retelling of events in a life—seems organic and even necessary. An obituary is a normative retelling and capturing of a life's narrative and follows a specific structure, but over time obituaries have also become indicators of social status rather than simply death notices. Obituaries, and the information contained within them, are limited by money (people pay per word or column inch for the newspaper space), and they usually feature those in control of the grieving discourse—the central players in the life of the deceased. In fact, obituaries, like the funeral services that follow them, reflect the social strata surrounding the deceased, listing in a very particular order the most important persons to the deceased. In the same way, funeral services also reflect this narrative—close family members sit in the front rows, then more distant family members, and, in the back, friends and acquaintances. Thus, traditional forms of mourning reflect a normative family structure, an ordering of the world surrounding the deceased that may look nothing like the actual world the deceased inhabited. Internet memorialization has turned this ordering on its head by allowing the mourning discourse of traditionally marginalized grievers to come to the fore. Not only has the Internet democratized the process of grieving (with both positive and negative results), but we are also finding a new set of traditions and mourning rituals emerging on the Internet that both complement and at times replace more traditional social structures of grieving.

Material Memorials and Their Virtual Counterparts

Many of the material memorials examined in this book have corresponding virtual memorials on the Internet, and almost all of them serve multiple functions: memorializing, raising awareness, encouraging political activism, or raising money. Ghostbike memorials memorialize individuals, provide publicity, raise money, and also provide a political platform for promoting safer regulations for cyclists. The Love & Hope Aurora memorial is a community Facebook page with over ten thousand members that seeks to create a physical memorial for those killed and to enact stronger gun control legislation in Colorado.[1] Nickel Mines, because it is in an Amish community that discourages memorialization, has no memorial page, but Sandy Hook Elementary has over ten memorial sites, seven on Facebook alone; the total of all members across these sites numbers more than a million.[2] Some car-decal and T-shirt memorials link, through a website address or a Quick Response (QR) code at the bottom of the design, to an Internet memorial as well. That being said, however, another connection between car-decal memorials and the Internet is the emerging practice of posting pictures of one's car-decal memorial on various support-group websites; in this way the websites offer another, perhaps more sympathetic audience for the car-decal memorials and their messages. Tattoos seem to be an exception here, though they are also heading in the direction of the Internet, as some tattoo artists ink QR codes into the tattoo.[3] Though QR code technology will soon be rendered obsolete by image recognition software, the newer software should make links to Internet memorials almost instantaneous, which will eliminate the need to actually tattoo a code on the skin and make the connection between the physical tattoo and the Internet site nearly immediate. In short, with technological advances, it will not be long before everything from tattoos to tombstones is physically linked to the Internet. What, then, does this mean for the future of grief and the understanding of death? Situating virtual memorials in the landscape of our imagination makes them no less real; we have removed the harsh realities of death and the limitations of bodies fixed in time and space, but the Internet allows these bodies once again to be transcribed on the geographies of our mind.

Deathscapes: The Funeral Industry and Memorialization

Commercial Internet memorials are sold with funeral packages in addition to the embalmment, visitation, and entombment or cremation. As part of a funeral or memorial package, the bereaved community is made a partner to the memorialization process and encouraged to write on the site and give offerings, both virtual and verbal, to the deceased. These Internet memorials are promoted as a way to be present at the actual funeral service if one cannot attend it, while also allowing the mourner to memorialize for posterity her or his feelings and thoughts about the deceased. Additionally, Internet memorials in the funeral industry help direct monetary contributions from the mourning community in the deceased person's memory, and they allow contributors to virtually "sign" the memorial, in addition to, or in lieu of, a guestbook at a funeral home. In this way, memorials can operate as a mourning space *beyond* that of the brick-and-mortar funeral home, which allows the bereaved to preserve their memories for future generations.

A survey of local funeral homes in Waco, Texas (a small college town often described as a "suburb" of Austin or Dallas), whose clientele includes the immediate community and outlying rural areas, found that funeral companies leading the trend in offering Internet memorials were either large industry franchises, such as Dignity Me-

morial, whose size allows it to offer Internet memorialization packages that include platform support at the national level,[4] or smaller,
family-owned operations trying to remain competitive in the local
market.[5] The older mom-and-pop funeral establishments did not generally offer Internet services as part of their packages, and some funeral home directors did not even know what these services were. As
funeral packages themselves are relatively new (before the U.S. government's deregulation of the funeral industry in the 1970s, it was
customary to sell services à la carte; it is only recently that entire funeral packages are bundled and sold together), it is not surprising that
some smaller, family-owned establishments have not caught up with
the larger corporations in offering Internet memorials as part of their
services. Additionally, the discrepancy in the use of Internet memorialization is in part influenced by external factors such as urban-rural
geographical divides and class lines. In areas where the clients are
younger, middle-class, and probably own a computer, Internet services tend to be more readily available and are more readily embraced.

More recent developments in the funeral industry include interac-
tive tombstones that allow the embedding of a barcode that is read by
a smartphone, which permits the bereaved to interact with the deceased through prerecorded video or audio clips, containing favorite
quotes or narratives predetermined by the deceased or selected by the
family for those visiting the grave site.[6] These barcodes allow visitors
to the grave site to access many of the stories and memories of the deceased within a virtual community of the bereaved, while simultaneously offering a space mirrored in virtual reality of the Real Life space.
Additionally, the barcodes offer a GPS location for the headstone itself. This offers the practical function of being able to use smart phone
technology to locate the tombstone with ease, and the ability to maintain a geographical relationship with the deceased.[7] These bar codes
and Internet links on tombstones are the first bridge between the physical and virtual realms. Located at the site of the buried or cremated
corpse, they link to a virtual realm where the dead remains alive
through video, pictures, conversations, and memories of the bereaved.

In mainland China, the Chinese government has initiated the
move to virtualizing the memorialization process; the Beijing Funeral
Supervision Department built an Internet memorialization service in

2004 for the city's seventeen cemeteries, offering mourners free online memorial services for the first seven years following a funeral service. Similar practices abound in Hong Kong, where the national cemetery offers Internet memorialization services as part of its the funeral package. The move in Hong Kong to sea burials as a way to extend land resources has created the need for virtual memorialization as a way to permit bereaved families to continue traditional memorial observances while not exhausting Hong Kong's limited resources on the dead.[8] Traditional Chinese mourning practices require a visit to the tomb at least once a year, with food offerings, the burning of incense, and the burning of symbolic goods that one might need in the afterlife, such as alcohol, phony paper money, or paper houses and cars. In addition, Chinese have traditionally practiced *Qingming*, the cleaning of the graves and offerings, observed on the 104th day after the winter solstice (or the fifteenth day after the spring equinox). The Chinese government has promoted Internet memorial services as part of a move to decrease travel expenses while also providing an environmentally green alternative to conducting ancestral offerings at the graves. The hope is to decrease actual physical migration during the *Qingming* period and to make it more culturally acceptable to make virtual offerings to the deceased. As Lily Kong has written, competition for land between the living and the dead has helped promote the practice of cremation in China, and now, "the need for locatedness of grief and memory in the physical world may be transcended by creating a virtual site in the on-line world."[9] Virtual mourning may be a way to transcend physical space in this world and, ultimately, possibly even material bodies themselves, by dislocating the grieving experience so that it is accessible virtually everywhere and not limited by geography. It is interesting to note, however, that it is sometimes geography itself that is pushing the move of death and grieving into a virtual realm, no longer necessitating the constraints (or benefits) of material physicality. In a world with decreasing land available, particularly for deathscapes, or areas where the dead are to be buried, virtual tombstones are one way to extend the physical realm.

In March 2011 Wang Guorong launched Shanghai's first memorial website, called Eternal Home, another government-sanctioned and -funded Internet application, along with a corresponding phone application with China Mobile, which has now become China's first SMS (Short Message Service or, in the vernacular, texting) mourning service. This application will increase virtual memorialization; services include offerings of incense and paper money, writing notes, playing songs, and even sending short text messages to the deceased, who are assigned their own phone number for receiving the memorial messages. As Wang, of the Shanghai Academy of Social Sciences, states, "'For those who can't make the pilgrimage, online tomb sweeping has relieved their burden of travelling and offers them a green and economical alternative to the traditional paper burning. . . . The virtual burning of incense does not pose the same challenge to the environment as in the real world.'"[10] Like the commercially driven funeral industry in the United States, the Chinese funeral business also is seeing the appeal of transitioning to a virtual world of memorializing the dead. In a country where land is at a premium and cremation is encouraged, virtual memorializing offers the opportunity to do *more* for the dead while supporting the Chinese government's drive for a greener, more sustainable environment.[11] With 31.6 percent of China's population of more than 1.3 billion using the Internet in 2010, and a government promoting virtual memorialization, the landscape of bereavement in China continues to evolve.[12]

Smart chips in tombstones and phone numbers for the deceased both offer ways to keep in touch with the deceased that are actually new, in that they help maintain a connection with the dead that is actively maintained and constantly carried with the grievers. It also allows the physical nature of the body to extend beyond the grave. If we can "visit" the dead at any point during the day, view their tombstones without actually leaving our houses or cars, and communicate with them at any point through their own phone numbers, then the material body is, in a way, less important. Though grieving individuals may have carried on private discourses with the dead in their heads or in personal journals for years, Internet memorialization allows both private and public discourse: it essentially makes public previously private language from the bereaved to the dead. Now, when one writes to the dead on a memorial web page or a social network memorial, one's personal and private thoughts are written for an audience, both known and anonymous. The very nature of Internet memorialization reveals two distinct factors: (1) the limited ability of funerary discourse to adequately express and ultimately address bereavement, and (2) the need, whether publicly sanctioned or not, for individuals to maintain some sort of relationship with the dead.

Extending the idea of memorialization is the creation of an "avatar in the afterlife," which captures the likeness and gestures of the deceased person that one can visit at any time online. These avatars are touted as a way to build an online legacy, or even to bring deceased ones back to life through socially constructed memory projects. The most popular websites currently building Internet avatars are called Lifenaut and Virtual Eternity, and they are geared expressly toward creating "life after death" on the Internet. Bruce Duncan, of the Terasem Movement Foundation, states on the Lifenaut Blog, "Helping people to come together around the building of an online biography and avatar about someone they care about can be fun! Imagine bringing your favorite great grandfather or auntie back to virtual life, using family history, old photos, videos and other digital reflections for sharing with future generations."[13] The success of the avatars remains to be seen, but the tombstone barcodes are already a reality. Following the earthquake and tsunami in 2011, the Japanese government ordered five hundred tombstones embedded with QR codes as a way to both memorialize the dead and warn the living.[14] Visits to the cemetery are shifting now into both a physical and virtual experience, and it should not be long before social media capture this as well. In the United States, however, visiting the actual physical site of the body after the burial is relatively rare, and the virtual memorial may not merely supplement the physical visitation, but supplant it.[15] In the case of virtual tombstones and virtual memorials, the body is virtually disappeared and replaced with a virtual reality in which the deceased lives on, or is at least occasionally remembered in ways that do not incorporate death as part of the experience.

Communal Grieving: Internet Sites as Intentional Spaces to Mourn

In addition to the commercial endeavors of virtual memorials directly associated with funeral companies, there is the construction of

popular virtual memorials (entrepreneurial *and* nonprofit) intentionally created for grieving communities. These online memorials serve
similar purposes, offering online support and community for the bereaved while constructing meaning out of death through public memory and life narratives. Whether in honor of a single person or a
community (e.g., parents of babies who have died from Sudden Infant
Death Syndrome—SIDS—or families of suicide victims), these memorials are seen as alternative spaces and additional avenues for
grieving, and most studies of these virtual memorials have noted
their general therapeutic value.[16] It is in response to these memorial
sites that the funeral industry began its own commercial version of
virtual memorials, and their popularity and functionality as support
groups reveal a continuing need for alternative grieving spaces online. The most recent type of memorial to emerge is the social network memorial, generally the Facebook or Myspace page of a person
who has died, which then becomes the locus of memorialization,
whereby a continuing contingent of the community remembers the
life and death of the deceased person. Since much has been written on
these communal bereavement sites, I want to turn now to examine
social network sites of memorialization, sites of mourning that often
seem to emerge spontaneously and are frequently seen as virtual sites
corresponding to material memorials.

Speaking to the Dead: Social Network Memorials

Social network memorials reveal an organic, popular, and uncen-
sored form of grieving that differs from intentionally or commercially constructed grief support sites. Social network memorials have
no recognizable power discourse, no web page moderator (besides
the site moderators, of course), or any tie to monetary gain (except
perhaps in preprogrammed social network pop-ups). They generally
emerge when a person who has a social network page dies, and those
who are "friends" or part of the social nexus of that site decide to
keep the page open for further commentary and discussion. What
often happens is that such pages become informal centers for mourning, and certain protocols regarding the deceased are usually followed, including posting one's picture with the deceased as one's

profile picture immediately following a death and on yearly anniver-saries, and messages are written on the deceased person's social net-work page to the dead person as if he or she were still alive. When social network memorials first emerged, Facebook and Myspace had no formal policies regarding what to do with pages of the deceased, but the overwhelming popularity of this type of memorialization has created the need for official company and legal policies for pages of the dead. When this phenomenon first occurred, family members and friends wanted to continue to have access to social network pages so they could continue to "visit the dead" and share memories of the deceased, as well as grieve in a public, yet intimate, forum together. Soon, however, glitches in these social networks' programs became evident, as "Internet ghosts" began to emerge.

These "ghosts" were essentially program-generated prompts that functioned as part of the social network application, such as the sug-gestion to "like" something or to "friend" somebody because one's friend is a friend of someone else. When these prompts occurred after a person was deceased, they created the notion of a virtual ghost that lingered around the Internet, acting on behalf of the deceased.[17] To respond to the proliferation of "ghosts" in the system, social net-works now memorialize individual web pages—essentially deactivat-ing a page from active status to a "dead" site that can be visited and perused, but no longer operates with computer-generated prompts and links to other user pages. This, in turn, though, creates issues of legality (who retains the right to access, view, and shut down infor-mation once someone has died?), and also causes difficulties for the organic grieving communities that have come to view these social network sites as "safe" places to conduct their mourning. For this reason, Facebook and Myspace created official policies regarding what happens to social network information once someone has died.[18] Generally, once an English-speaking user has died, Facebook, Myspace, or Google+ memorializes the user's site by adding the let-ters RIP (Rest in Peace), which lets other users know that the site now belongs to a deceased person and is no longer formally active. Chi-nese-speaking sites use a "V" (in place of the "V" hand gesture for peace), and Spanish-speaking sites use the acronym DEP (Descanse en Paz) or the English RIP. Thus, interestingly enough, across different cultures and languages similar titles are used, and the strategy remains the same: the web page is kept active for the benefit of the bereaved, but its status is shifted to that of a memorial so that Internet users are no longer plagued by "ghosts" and legal issues can be circumvented as quickly as possible. Internet memorialization, because of its user interface, seems to be contributing to the syntax of memorialization in its own way, contributing to the effects of globalization.

The legal issues for memorializing pages have spawned a whole new generation of companies geared to the management of virtual information after death, and companies like these are among the faster-growing industries on the Internet.[19] Because of the proliferation of spontaneous memorials, and the growing practice of mourning online on someone's defunct site, social networks have also generated extended memorial services that have begun to grow in popularity as sites for the bereaved. For example, Myspace has spawned "MyDeathSpace," which released its first smartphone application on January 29, 2012.[20] MyDeathSpace is essentially a spinoff of Myspace, but for those who have died. There the grieving post obituaries, newspaper articles, and other information about those who have died, which others can then visit and post their thoughts and comments. MyDeathSpace differs from spontaneous memorials in that it serves as a repository of death and is not focused on one individual, and it is similar to Myspace in its younger audience: it generally highlights accidental deaths and suicides, rather than deaths from old age or disease. It may seem to some macabre in its emphasis on death rather than remembering and memorializing, but to others it is comforting in its assertion that death is universal, no matter what age or class.[21] As technology continues to expand, memorialization endures, and the repertoire of Internet memorialization services is expanding to keep up with the growing demand for a virtual life after death.

These spontaneous Internet memorial sites are not limited to the English-speaking web. In China a site called Kids Who Go to Heaven is a collection of Internet memorials, photos, epitaphs, and stories of the deceased in one online album on renren.com, a Chinese-language site. The site, started by a twenty-two-year-old named He Dan, has received mixed reviews, as some friends and families cherish the In-

ternet afterlives of their loved ones, and others have seen it as an inva-
sion of privacy. He Dan states, "Friends and family of the deceased
can visit their loved ones' profiles when they miss them. I often do
this and leave messages for my friend who passed away."[22] Like
MyDeathSpace, however, Kids Who Go to Heaven continues to draw
visitors and has received several million hits since its inception in
June 2011.

Much like Facebook, Renren is a social network site popular
among Chinese middle school, high school, and university students,
currently claiming around 31 million active monthly users, that has
encountered similar issues regarding the deaths of its users. Originally an application (much like Facebook) for establishing one's identity
and status among fellow students, the application was known as *Xiao-
nei* (school insiders), but it soon changed its name to Renren wang, or
the people's net, to encompass a larger public, and it is making strides
in the overseas Chinese population as well, as Chinese students travel
abroad. Renren and other social network sites in China are different
from those in the United States because they operate under strict cen-
sorship by the Chinese government. Microblogging sites (such as Sina
Weibo, which started in 2009 and claimed 300 million registered users as of February 2012) and other social media sites today provide
one of the fastest and most far-reaching forms of social protest among
student groups and other organizations that wish to criticize the Chinese government. Deaths, like funeral ceremonies in ancient China,
still act as a major platform through which criticism of the Chinese
government is publically sanctioned and somewhat tolerated. One recent example is the deaths in July 2011 of Xiang Yu'an and Shi Li-
hong in the fatal train wreck in Wenzhou, Zhejiang province.[23]
Following Xiang's and Shi's deaths, their Renren accounts were memorialized, receiving unprecedented numbers of hits and visitors
seeking to use the memorials as a platform not only to remember
Xiang and Shi, but also to criticize the Chinese government for its al-
leged materialism, corruption, and inefficiency. Though Xiang and
Shi are unusual examples, Renren accounts, like those on Facebook
and Myspace, are regularly turned into spontaneous memorials for
the bereaved and grieving, where mourning is given a public space for
expression.

The Chinese government sometimes tolerates (within limits) the political protest generated by Internet memorials, but in Latin America virtual memorials intentionally focus on political mobilization; pages for social justice movements function as hubs of information dissemination and memory building. Examples of these political memorials are sites such as Proyecto Desaparecidos, which focuses primarily on victims of governmental injustice in Latin America, and the site of Carlos Mugica, a priest killed in the 1970s in Argentina whose family and friends are seeking his official recognition as a martyr.[24] These sites are memorials geared toward a particular audience in recognition of a political aim, but there are also examples of Internet memorials that double as support networks for victims of homicide, suicide, or SIDS, as there are on the English-speaking web.

Latin American social network memorials also abound. Latin America is similar to its northern counterpart in its use of social network platforms: 96 percent of its population logs on to social network sites on a regular basis. In fact, Argentina is second only to Israel in the number of hours its citizens spend online at social network sites, particularly Facebook.[25] Spontaneous memorials in Latin America, like their English and Chinese counterparts, emerge following a person's death and then operate as centers of support for the bereaved, besides offering information concerning funeral and memorial ceremonies. There does *not* seem to be, however, a general awareness or concern about virtual information following one's death in Latin America, as there is in North America, but Facebook's move into the Latin American market is also relatively recent.

In all these virtual memorials across cultures (both in communal grieving sites and in social network memorials), however, one feature is saliently similar, and that is the mourning discourse used by the bereaved to express their grief online. On Facebook and on Renren, grieving rituals are interestingly alike, and a new form of grieving—on the Internet—has emerged. It is common to find a remembrance of the dead on the Internet, including a picture of the bereaved with the deceased that confirms the bereaved's relationship and familiarity with the dead. In short, it says, "I knew her. We were close." And as the anthropologist Donald Joralemon has pointed out, it also reveals one's status as bereaved: changing one's status picture to a photo of oneself with the deceased is a visual marker, simultaneously honoring the dead (like the previous wearing of a black armband), and telling one's social circle, "I am grieving. I am a mourner. *This* is my status." Additionally, grieving rituals have emerged in these social networks: the marking of each anniversary with a reposting of the picture ("Remember, I am still grieving"), and writing (if the page is still available) to the deceased on his or her own page.[26] Similarly, the funeral industry, whether in the United States, China, Japan, or Latin America, is similarly driving the trend toward a global grief discourse on its virtual memorial platforms. Though the prayers may differ in content, as may the gods the prayers are being directed to, and the gifts offered to honor the dead may shift across countries, the essential software is the same, and the ways in which people both honor and speak to or about the dead are virtually the same, whether in English, Chinese, Japanese, or Spanish. Memorialization as observed in social network sites, and as practiced in funeral industry memorial programs, is being driven largely by software applications and the ways in which the memorial programs are constructed for user interface, but they are spurring a larger global trend of memorialization that is erasing cultural and linguistic barriers when it comes to remembering and thinking about the dead.

One exception to this trend is notable: the absence in both Asia and Latin America of Internet memorials that correspond with material memorials. In Latin America roadside memorials have been fairly common, and famous examples are found in Mexico, Colombia, and Argentina, but these roadside memorials do not extend to the virtual realm, as they often do in the United States and in some parts of Europe. Internet memorialization (such as that discussed previously) seems to be geared toward political activism, as Internet memorials are used to promote either social or political change, or provide grief support, and thus far have not been widely connected to, or seen as an extension of, other material memorials. In Japan and China gravestone Internet memorialization is popular and encouraged, but one does not find mass spontaneous material memorialization at the grassroots level, or such things as car decals, tattoos, and T-shirts announcing one's status as bereaved. This may be, in part, due to the fact that religious memorialization in Japan and China already incorporates material memorialization as a part of its rituals of remembrance. In fact, the Internet memorials attached to gravestones in both China and Japan have largely been sponsored by the government to address broader social needs (such as land shortages and traffic patterns) rather than driven by a desire for individual memorialization. In short, though Internet memorials exist in both Latin America and Asia, the connections between material memorials and corresponding Internet memorials there either seem to be initiated in the United States (in examples such as the ghostbike memorials and their website) or are not that common, though further research needs to be done to examine this phenomenon in depth.[27] Though the language and syntax used and found in Internet memorials seem very similar across cultures, the link between material memorials and Internet memorials as extensions of one another seems mostly limited to the United States and Europe.

Discourses of the Dead: Obituaries, Eulogies, and Social Remembrance

The very public nature of the funeral ceremony is reflected in the formal language used, whereby the function of the funeral is to mark a shift in the dead person's status from alive to dead, from community participant to historical person, which is accomplished through a retelling of the person's biography, so that the deceased's life is constructed into a neatly packaged narrative that simultaneously makes sense and constructs meaning. Obituaries are the hallmark of this biographic retelling of a life, the narrative reconstruction of life after death. Obituaries and the accompanying funerary discourse are concerned with constructing a biography, a narrative, and an understanding of a life through its retelling. An analysis of funerary language, Christian or Jewish, Chinese or Spanish, finds the essential formulas strikingly similar. Though the rituals of honoring, remembering, and grieving the dead differ across cultures, the function of the biographic retelling is similar: a life is tidily constructed, and death is the end of the story. The third-person voice is used in telling the story of the deceased: relationships, hobbies, and achievements are catalogued, and the past tense is used, placing the person firmly in the past. This life is over, and the community comes together to acknowledge and lament that fact.

In regard to the function of biography, Geoffrey Harpham writes, "The effect of mimesis is to displace and so stabilize the wandering subject, to humble human pretensions to autonomy by submitting life to the rules of grammar, rhetoric, and generic convention. . . . Textuality constitutes an ascesis, a deadening, a purging of materiality and mutability."[28] Biographies attempt to impose a narrative structure to a life and give meaning to it, but obituaries place boundaries on a life, underscoring not only the life as narrative, as fixed point, but also situating the deceased within a fixed social structure. The function of obituaries in American culture has shifted in the last hundred years. Traditionally, obituaries had the dual role of notifying the public of the death and giving the details of the upcoming funeral or memorial service; they differed from eulogies, which were speeches of praise and memories about a deceased individual. Now, however, obituaries sometimes take the place of a service, and they can read like a eulogy.

Obituaries reveal just as much about the audience constructing it as they do about the deceased, locating the deceased not just in time but in a fixed social space. In this way the dead person (and, by extension, those mourning that death) is fixed in a web of personal and social relationships neatly outlined in the obituary. Details included and facts omitted in an obituary narrative not only become crucial points to understanding how a person's life is viewed by a community, but also reveal much about the audience attached to that specific, refracted memory. In reality, however, obituaries can rarely serve as "objective" retellings of a person's life; most often, though it is not always acknowledged, the narrative construction of a person's life is given meaning and organization that is rarely noticed in the messy boundaries of life itself. Additionally, these narrative reconstructions of lives marginalize grievers who may have been central to the deceased. The natal family is nearly always given privilege in the structure of grieving, though in reality the deceased may no longer have had close ties to that natal family, and may have, in fact, been closer to his or her network of friends or religious community. Obituaries often serve, then, if not intentionally, to reinforce the ties of the deceased to their families of origin. Thus, Internet memorialization, and the new virtual rituals emerging as part of it, can be seen to democratize mourning, circumventing traditional and hierarchical notions of family and social structure. This democratization has led to disruptions of traditional social ways of interacting both with the dead and with the mourning community itself.

Internet Syntax: The Language of Virtual Memorials

There are several rituals that have emerged in Internet mourning; these rituals seem to be universally practiced, though they may in fact go against traditional cultural ways of observing mourning. They are in part defined by the user interface of the social networks themselves. In other words, the syntax we use in Internet mourning is defined, limited, and perpetuated by the software applications that we are using to memorialize. Several popular practices in social network memorialization are (1) the posting of a photo of oneself with the deceased as one's profile picture, and then the regular reposting of that photo to commemorate anniversaries of the death and birthdays of the deceased; and (2) the writing of messages to the deceased—often frequently at first, and then at regular intervals that mark the deceased's birthday and anniversary of death. The posting of photos of oneself with the deceased serves several functions—to demonstrate to the community that one knew the deceased and that the loss is personal and that one has the right to mourn the deceased. It is, essentially, very similar to wearing mourning clothing or a black armband. It is a desire for recognition as bereaved. Posting a photo of oneself with the deceased essentially tells the virtual community that "I am in mourning" and grants one the space to write, reflect, and think about the deceased. It is a personal expression of grief within a community that does not require time off from work or an immediate response. Additionally, posting such a photo immediately grants one the social capital to claim one's bereaved status without marking that status hierarchically.

Though I previously discussed how these new rituals of virtual mourning can democratize the grieving process and give a voice to those who have been traditionally marginalized in the grieving process, this "leveling out" is not always desirable or welcome. One widow I interviewed felt that, in her particular situation, the social network memorial excluded her and did not privilege her status as "primary mourner." She said that she felt she should have received sympathy cards for the loss of her husband, but that in her husband's social network memorial, "everyone" felt the need to share her or his grief and memories of her husband, and no one seemed to recognize her pain. Additionally, she didn't want people writing to her dead husband, but writing to her and offering condolences.[29] Clearly, the widow wanted her hierarchical status in the real world to extend to the virtual realm, and she was unhappy with the Internet's democratizing process. No less important, however, was the fact that the widow didn't understand why people were writing to her husband, who was dead, and not writing to her. For the widow the social network memorial functioned much like Derrida's ghost—its presence haunted her as a specter of what is no longer present. The social network memorial site was not a source of comfort to her but a reinforcement of her husband's absence. The site was no longer her husband's, nor was it hers—it was now a public space for others to speak about her husband. The absence of her husband was a real and physical presence, and the virtual realm was an almost mocking of his absence—which seemed to bring others comfort, but only made her husband's absence even greater. As Derrida writes about Roland Barthes:

> Even if I wanted or was able to give an account, to speak of him as he was for me (the voice, the timbre, the forms of his attention and distraction, his polite way of being there or elsewhere, his face, hands, clothing, smile, his cigar, so many features I name without describing, since this is impossible here), even if I try to reproduce what took place, what place would be reserved for the reserve? What place for the long periods of silence, for what was left unsaid out of discretion, for what was of no use bringing up, either because it was too well known by both of us or else infinitely unknown on either side? To go on speaking of this all alone, after the death of the other, to sketch out the least conjecture or risk the least interpretation, feels to me like an endless insult or wound—and yet also a duty, a duty toward him.

Yet, I will not be able to carry it out, at least not right here.
Always the promise of return.[30]

Derrida here refers to the absence of Barthes and how, try as he might, that absence can never be filled or completely recollected; the silences, the gestures—they are all missing, and words cannot bring these things back to life. The Internet makes this issue even more pressing—as the bereaved are confronted with not only memories, but also pictures, videos, and comments about the deceased person's daily life.

Social networks can operate as a sort of time capsule, with the option to go back to view past posts and comments. Facebook's "Timeline" format is just such an illustration of this capability, in which postings become a virtual chronology of events.[31] The disruption to a person's timeline by death helps explain the continuity in language on the social network memorial. In some way the deceased is still "present" through this access to the recent past, and thus the language used by the mourning community often reflects this way of thinking. The bereaved explain to the deceased how his or her death has affected them, and they often tell the dead intimate details, revealing dreams, visions, and other more private experiences, such as what life feels like without the deceased. This is strikingly different from the discourse of funerals and public mourning rituals, in which formal language is employed and the deceased is generally referred to in the third person and the past tense, which emphasizes the distance of the mourners from the deceased. In social network memorials, though occasionally the more formal funerary language is employed, more often mourners tend to use instead the second person and the present continuous tense, as though the deceased were still alive and they were in conversation with the deceased. Time also becomes blurred, as posters can essentially go back in time and respond to a deceased person's post even though that person has died. A conversation interrupted can be responded to and changed and the original interaction altered. Derrida's promise of return here is never-ending, and the widow is forced to watch a conversation with her husband continue without him.

Whereas obituaries generally use language *about* the dead, social network language differs in that it is more often language written *to* the dead.[32] In this way, social network memorials resemble newspaper notices commemorating an anniversary of a death, in which someone celebrates a Mass for the deceased or publishes a notice in a newspaper remembering that person. These notices, or memoriams, tend to be more common in Catholic communities; like social networks, they employ language that is at once familiar and intimate. Often memoriams give the person's name, birth and death dates, and a short message from the living to the dead, sometimes accompanied by a notice for a commemorative Mass in honor of the deceased. Messages are usually deeply personal, while also claiming social recognition of the grieving status of the bereaved. One example is this memoriam recently published in the *Waco Tribune-Herald*:

> Yolanda, it's been 7 years and I'm still in love with you and miss you so much.
> Mom, you will never know the many things you have taught us. To love, laugh, to worship, to be fearless, and so much more. We wish we could hug you and thank you. We Love and Miss you so much.
> Love, Irie, Friend, Sonya, Israel, and grandkids
> May 4, 1957–April 25, 2006[33]

The language here is deeply similar to that used in social network sites, including the use of the second person and the present tense. In Spanish these notices are called *recordatorios* and serve the same function. Here is one from *La Nacion*, one of the principal newspapers of Argentina: "Raiman, Laura—At ten years from your departure, we miss you profoundly and express our eternal love to your memory. Your parents Hilda and Federico, your siblings, Nora and Horacio, your in-laws Karina and Ricardo, and your nieces Candela, Victoria and Lucia, who, even though they never knew you, have you present in their lives."[34]

In Spanish the language is the same—informal and intimate—but one similarity between these notices and obituaries remains—the situating of the dead within their social complexes. The social network of relationships is replicated here, in ways that are not found online in social media sites. Perhaps these notices can be seen as a sort of bridge between obituaries and social network mourning; they contain the same informal and intimate language as the latter, but they are generally still written by, paid for, and published by and for the family. It is a way for the family to honor the dead while informing the wider community that these anniversaries are significant. Simultaneously, these newspaper notices mark, for many, major milestones in the grieving process. I have seen notices that mark six months, one, two, three, and ten or even twenty years.

Language in social network memorials, though, is even more informal than that used in these memoriam notices; it reflects spoken language as well as that generally used in texts and brief e-mail messages. (There is often the written substitution of letters for words prevalent in everyday text communication—"r" for *are,* "u" for *you.*) This reflects the generally spontaneous nature of the communication initiated from the bereaved to the deceased, but it also reveals the trend of using smart phones to initiate and conduct communication in a quick and truncated manner. Emoticons and symbols reflecting emotions are also used, further punctuating the grammar of memorializing online. It is not enough to say "I miss you," but rather "I miss u :(" or even "I miss u :_(" or "T_T"[35] when writing messages to the deceased. The emoticon of a face with tears or a sad face reveals more than simply the message, and it is not limited by a formal grieving discourse or proper modes of expression. The informal and intimate language of social network memorials that use the present continuous tense when speaking to the deceased rejects the formal past tense of funerary and obituary discourse, even when the mourners themselves were not intimate with the person they are grieving. If one looks only at the language when examining social network memorials, it is often difficult to discern the social relationships between the bereaved and the deceased. This may reflect a larger social and cultural trend toward more informal modes of expression in general, but it is a shift nonetheless. When a famous person dies today, or a traumatic social event occurs resulting in the death of a person, the language used to memorialize that person is the same—informal and appropriating.

One recent example of this phenomenon is the page memorializing the death of Krystle Campbell, one of the people killed in the bombings at the Boston Marathon. Her page was created one day after the Boston bombings, and nearly ten days later it had 75,984 "likes" on Facebook, and nearly 205,478 people had discussed the page or left comments on her photos.[36] Comments on Campbell's page vary, but most offer condolences to her family, discuss the tragedy of the events, or speak to Campbell herself. What is interesting, however, is the use of extremely informal language, emoticons, and shortened words even by those who do not seem to have known her personally.

Rosanne DeGustino Monaco
So beautiful, so sad . . . R.I.P Angel Girl. . . . sigh. . . .

Laurie Poland
Beautiful so sorry honey u will be missed RIP.
19 hours ago via mobile

In the second comment, the writer has used her cellphone to post her message to the deceased. Similar types of language are found in nearly every social network site, from those that are open to a very limited group of friends to those mourning the famous. These sites seem to provide, in some form, a sense of Victor Turner's concept of *communitas,* providing a place where individuals can come together as mourners outside traditionally accepted norms of bereavement and grieving structures and grieve their loss in a way that helps them understand and construct meaning out of death. As Turner asserts, "People have a real need to doff the masks, cloaks and apparel and insignia of status from time to time even if only to don the liberating masks of a liminal masquerade."[37] On social network sites, people are able to simultaneously claim the cloak of grieving, asserting their role as grief bearers, and step outside the traditional confines of a society that determines who, how, why, and how long to grieve. This can be done, however, while assuming an alternative identity online—Turner's "masks" are simply extensions of self in the virtual realm. One can mourn online in chat rooms and social network sites, while continuing one's daily life.

Examining the vast numbers on Internet sites constructed to memorialize the dead—over a million for the Sandy Hook shootings,
76,000 for Krystle Campbell—reveals the need for memorialization
that circumvents traditional mourning hierarchies. The Internet both
democratizes grieving and allows an extension of who can grieve the
dead. Erika Doss, in her book *Memorial Mania,* points to the "obses-
sion with issues of memory and history and an urgent desire to express and claim those issues in visibly public contexts."[38] It is not
merely a desire to mourn, but a desire to mourn in a public and visible
sphere—to be recognized and belong to a group that is mourning—
and to make meaning out of death. Indeed, the mourning conducted
on the Internet in many ways reflects Daniel Boorstin's theory of consumption communities—communities based on similar affective responses to consumerism.[39] But in this case it is the communal response
to death, and the desire to mourn in a similar fashion, that creates
these online communities. The craving to belong to an extensive network may partly drive these grieving websites. The democratization
of death, then, operates on dual levels. On the one hand, grieving online challenges traditional social structures operative in mourning rituals while, on the other hand, it allows mourners to belong to a
consumption community marked by its identity as bereaved. This is
borne out by sites such as the ones established following the Boston
Marathon explosions and the shootings in Newtown, Connecticut.
Membership in these social network grieving sites expanded exponentially within the first weeks of the traumatic events and extended
far beyond the geographical boundaries of the events themselves.
Though other groups may be marked by a similar taste in beer or an
appetite for organic food, the consumption community here is not
about death but about mourning and a shared identity of grief.

Though death rituals and language differ cross-culturally, the
bereavement language on the Internet, surprisingly, varies little. Internet bereavement reveals a metalanguage that seems to supersede
local culture. In China, for example, not only are there similar tools
to express mourning and connect those grieving, but even the language used in spontaneous memorials is also more familiar and informal. In Xiamen, a Fujian province netizen writes in the aftermath
of a train crash:

Two of my friends were on the train. One of them has come back with limitless sorrow, while the other in heaven wishes us the best from heaven. I cry without tears now, how much she loved her motherland, always scolding weak me for wanting to emigrate, for wanting to flee, but now, she doesn't understand why even they will still lie in the face of the entire world about something so impossible to conceal as death and casualty numbers. . . . I feel helpless, I feel angry, our goodness/kindness is slowly being strangled/stifled. I look up towards the heavens and shout angrily, let the storm come more fiercely![40]

Here the writer switches back and forth between the past and present tenses in describing her deceased friend, explaining how the past actions of her dead friend now affect the current emotions of her friend in her afterlife, as well as her own feelings of helplessness as she moves forward with her new view of life and government.

One finds similar language used by Spanish speakers: it is informal, expressed in the second person and present continuous tense:

You are unique J . . . you didn't deserve this . . . But the guy who did this to you is going to pay dearly. We love you very much!!! You will always be in our hearts ♥ I didn't know you well, but well enough to know that you are a good person. . . . How much I am going to miss you. . . . ;(((Rest in peace. . . . We love you ♥ J——(08/20/11)[41]

E—— I cannot believe that this happened to you. I will not tell you good-bye because you will always be everyone's heart that knows you. (08/11/11)[42]

The spontaneous memorial discourse is strikingly similar across cultures in these Internet memorials, undercutting other research on cross-cultural mourning and grieving. Though I do not intend to posit here that there are not cultural differences, I am still surprised at many of the similarities in the Internet discourse of mourning, and I do suggest that perhaps the Internet offers its own "cultural language" regarding mourning that the bereaved are adopting. Just as local economies find themselves becoming part of a global market, and the McDonaldization of culture is undercutting local traditions, Internet discourse, and the ways in which the Internet and software applications frame communication, is shifting understandings of mourning into a global arena, as well.

The Internet itself has its own accepted linguistic code, which is changing and shaping the ways in which we speak about and, ultimately, view death, the afterlife, and the dead. The linguist David Crystal speaks of the modifications to language that the Internet has brought, such as shifts in style, neologisms, and slight changes in punctuation, but this language goes deeper than that, in the sense that we are seeing, particularly in social network memorials across cultures and different languages, a similar pattern of talking to and about the dead. This is not to say that old ways of speaking about the dead (using the third person and the past tense, describing our relationship with the dead in a biographic formula in a way that situates us in the present and the dead in our past) do not exist on the Internet; they do, and they are present alongside the voices that place the dead here with us now, on the receiving end of our communications. The Internet, and its virtual reality, offers an alternative way of seeing death and its role in our lives—a way that may be publicly sanctioned if not publicly acknowledged. The alternative realities we all inhabit online as "other" also allow for a discourse of death that in everyday discourse is too strange to acknowledge and condone but that many secretly hope for.[43] The dead somehow remain present online, whether through their past postings and their continuing timelines, or through computer-generated prompts that make them seem still among the living, and it is this very presence that may explain part of the appeal of social network memorialization. The dead do not seem as though they are absent—except perhaps, as discussed earlier in the case of the widow, for those for whom the absence is all too present.

Internet memorials also reveal a sharp distinction between public and private mourning discourses as they are practiced today, which prompts me to wonder if people must create their own private mourning discourses because they either are not readily available in public forums or are too exclusive. Though the Internet is actually a public forum, the language used in memorials reflects private conversation or thought, which is then publically shared. Internet mourning language is simultaneously public and private. Its function, however, is *not* to construct biographies or narrative understandings of a life, but to continue the conversation with the dead and acknowledge one's ongoing relationship with the person in his or her new status as deceased. Additionally, it is not only that public discourse intersects with private thought or expression, but also that past events seem to intersect with present and future in such a way that time itself is blurred. The public-private and present-past nature of virtual discourse allows traditional constructions of time to be blurred, so that the past, present, and future are no longer rigid divisions, but socially malleable (and socially condoned) distinctions. In the same way that physical space is transcended by virtual memorialization, and bodies become secondary to the memory of the individual, time is no longer the rigid distinction made in real life. Online, one can go back in time, viewing pictures, reading status updates, and watching videos posted by and about the deceased. Thus, past and present collide in a way that cannot occur in any other form (except perhaps for dreams) and yet is socially condoned. This malleable construction of time may in fact contribute to the language used in social networks and help explain its different voice and tense. The function of the social network memorial is not to place the person firmly in the past or impose a narrative structure, as the biography or obituary does. It is simply a way to maintain a relationship with the dead. It is like a time capsule message written to someone in the future; the audience is someone we believe is listening and interested in what we have to say. The audience is not us, but the dead.

Additionally, social network memorials function as memory spaces for the dead. As the Internet memorial is simultaneously public and private, present and past, it operates as a memory space that is not necessarily linear or chronological. In many ways social network memorials more accurately reflect lives than do their distant narrative cousins, obituaries. They are repositories of quips, funny moments and sayings, embarrassing and revealing pictures and passages, songs, and passing thoughts. They are *not* neatly structured, organized, or packaged, and so perhaps they more

closely resemble lives as they are: disorganized, without a clear purpose, full of sudden beginnings and endings, and containing no
clearly laid-out path. Essentially, they may serve as repositories that
most closely resemble our own jumble of memories, including spaces and gaps and a lack of a clear narrative trajectory. Perhaps the
private mourning process is better aided by life's messiness than the
neat package of death.

The frequent references in the various Internet memorial services
to virtual avatars and information protection agencies also reinforce
the notion of a "virtual afterlife." Even the *names* of Internet memorial services reflect a need to extend life rather than understand or
prepare for death. It is an important distinction—between Internet
afterlife as an extension of life (and denial of death) and the acceptance of death as final—that reflects a particular trend in the function of memorialization. The focus in commercial Internet memorials
tends to be on extending life and denying death, rather than on cop-
ing with and making sense of death. This focus may reflect cultural
shifts in attitudes toward death and dying. Simultaneously, however,
there is an emergence of both spontaneous mourning sites for communities with particular concerns (survivors of suicide, for example)
and social network sites that once belonged to the living but have become centers of bereavement, which offer a glimpse into the public-
private world of grieving on the Internet. Language in these
spontaneous memorials is dramatically different from traditional funerary and obituary discourse, dismissing the third person and the
past tense, and embracing instead the second person and the present
continuous tense, which are at once intimate and informal and reflect
a relationship between the living and the dead; this language is almost completely at odds with the publicly sanctioned language of funerals and memorials.

Mourning in public and taking time off from work to mourn are
not generally embraced, and our cultural view of mourning has shifted so that much of the bereavement literature in the field of psychology is concerned with defining and recognizing "excessive" grieving.
Though medicine has made many advances in prolonging life, people
today can no longer publicly self-identify, either as individuals or as
part of a community, as bereaved. The disappearance of the bereaved

from our communities mirrors the disappearance of dead bodies and their unsightly decay, and spontaneous memorials provide a public forum where the bereaved can continue to maintain their identity as grievers and feel that it is acceptable to mourn.[44]

5

Grieving the Dead in Alternative Spaces

Transactional Grieving and the Appropriation of the Dead

From the dead body to the virtual body and from material memorials to virtual memorials, one thing is clear: the bodiless nature of memorialization of the dead across cultures. There is a move to replacing the body with something else in order to remember the dead. In postindustrial, Protestant, and capitalist societies such as the United States (and Western Europe, though it is not covered in this book), this trend seems much more prominent and is moving at a faster rate than it is in the developing world. This is occurring for a variety of factors. Death is being denied through the disappearance of the body, by embalmment or cremation. Though embalmment and cremation occur in other societies, the interaction in those societies with the dead body before embalmment and cremation is much more involved. For example, in India the oldest child is expected to light the funeral pyre and begin the cremation of the deceased parent, whereas in Japan the oldest child accompanies the body to the crematorium and pushes the button to begin the burning of the body. In both instances, the family is actively involved in the cremation process, but in the United States people often die in a hospital and are then sent to a morgue, and then to the crematorium. There is little interaction with the dying, the dead, or the burial process. As globalization and industrialization increase, traditional cultural values and norms will be further eroded, and the trend toward bodiless memorialization will only intensify. Additionally, as the world's population and accompanying land scarcity continue to increase, the body as corpse will continue to disappear as countries look for new and innovative ways to dispose of the dead. Ultimately, the rise of memorialization is concurrent with the disappearance of the body.

Though not all cultures practice the same types of memorialization (for example, tattoo memorials are not prevalent in cultures that do not approve of tattooing), several commonalities appear. There seems to be a move across various cultures to replace the body in some form with a material or virtual reminder of the deceased. This desire to replace the missing body reveals a need for the living to maintain some sort of relationship with the dead. These memorials include various religious traditions, such as the Chinese Confucian tradition of replacing the missing body with a tablet that represents the deceased person, and, in Japan, the Buddhist memorial altar placed in the home and given daily offerings of incense, candles, prayers, and food. One well known example is the Mexican Day of the Dead ceremony, in which the dead are reinscribed in the world through a photo or an artistic rendering and given offerings and celebrated each year on All Saints Day and All Souls Day (November 1–2). In all these traditions, there is a transactional element between the living and the dead, symbolizing the need to keep the dead involved in the world of the living. Judaism, Islam, Chinese religions, Japanese Buddhism, and Roman Catholicism all have religious rituals that recognize the need to inscribe the dead onto the world of the living, whether through proscriptions against cremation (Judaism and Islam) and regular acts of memorialization,[1] through material objects such as ancestor tablets and altars, or even in the religious imagination of the dead through a world of saints, martyrs, and the regular intercession by and for the dead. The trend toward memorialization, both material and virtual, is a popular response to this universal need to continue to keep the dead in the realm of the living. Whether offerings left at the material memorials of shootings or at ghostbike memorials, or virtual candles and teddy bears given to the dead on Internet memorials, these interactions, both religious and popular, reveal the ongoing transactional nature of the relationship between the living and the dead.

The dead need to inhabit the world through their absence if they

The outpouring of grief at the Boston Marathon memorial included notes to the deceased, flowers, balloons, and hundreds of shoes. iStockphoto

are no longer present. Ghostbikes, for example, use white in their symbolic rendering of a phantom—attempting to re-create the image of a bike and thereby a ghostly apparition of a biker once present. Gifts and notes to the dead reveal this need as well; at the Boston Marathon memorial, running shoes, notes, teddy bears, and flowers, among other things, were left for the dead. These offerings were not merely symbolic; they were physical offerings to the dead that the living felt the dead would recognize and appreciate. Similarly, in Newtown, Connecticut, many left balloons, teddy bears, and flowers for the children who had been killed. These were not given to the grieving families of the deceased children, but to the dead children themselves, material symbols that the world of the living was still caring for the dead children. A part of mourning is this very transactional element of the relationship between the living and the dead. Social network and Internet memorials operate similarly—posting pictures of the dead, writing messages to them, and giving virtual gifts of candles, teddy bears, and so on to the deceased are all ways in which the bereaved can continue their relationship with the dead in a publicly accepted and acknowledged way. The objects for the dead, though, are not memento mori but objects of life. They are, in many ways, very similar to items used in the Chinese and Japanese tradition of giving food offerings to the dead; they fulfill the desire of the living to continue to care for and nurture the dead. In this way, the recent trend of memorialization is somehow different from the long-standing practice of roadside memorialization, or even of the MADD stickers, in which the purpose is to give the living a warning through the actions of the dead. Contemporary memorialization seeks somehow to sustain a relationship with the deceased. The dead have gone missing, and memorialization brings them back.

Space, Place, and Time

Popular memorialization also reveals the need to appropriate space, place, and time for the griever's needs. Rituals, such as the regular reposting of pictures of the deceased on anniversaries of deaths, are ways in which the bereaved are able to mark the calendar and highlight the importance of particular days. This reappropriation of time is not unlike the religious reenactment of the holy year through regular rituals such as the Hajj or the Lenten season. There is, however, a constant tension between these individual appropriations of time and space when they are located in the public sphere, and, as is the case with roadside memorials,[2] the public and the state are forced to deal with the political consequences of these individual appropriations. When people do not have adequate space and time in which to mourn the dead, they are forced to create new rituals that allow them to do so. Some religions around the world have incorporated mourning practices into their traditions (sitting shiva in Judaism, the mourning period of Japanese Buddhism, the Day of the Dead in Mexican Catholicism), but when these practices are no longer available in one's religious or cultural milieu, or when these practices are not highly valued in society, then individuals, in the decline or absence of these rituals, appropriate aspects of religious mourning rituals and cobble together new forms of mourning. The appropriation of mourning rituals and the creation of new forms of mourning are not entirely secular, and often they complement existing cultural and religious forms of mourning. Borrowing aspects of rituals previously only part of the religious realm allows individuals to create meaning out of death and reach their own highly personalized public expression of mourning.

Time, and the way it is understood, is most clearly reflected in these mourning rituals, and cultural differences in the relationship of time to the dead becomes evident. The mourning rituals of China, Japan, and Mexico all acknowledge the importance of the past, and of history in general. In Asia dead ancestors are given their place in the family history through established rituals and tablets that become part of the ancestral home. Ancestors are nourished because they form a link between past and present. In Mexico the annual Day of the Dead festival celebrates the dead with photos and altars in the homes. In contrast, American culture, through its banishment of the dead, reflects its future orientation to a new extreme. Bereaved Americans attempt to "move forward," "get over it," and "heal." The emphasis, even in mourning language, is not—as it is in the Chinese and Japanese contexts—on fixing the present through its relationship to the past, but rather on the future recovery from loss. Recovery in the American context, however, is not a recovery *of* the dead, but recovering *from* the death itself. Alan Dundes's seminal essay on future orientation resonates more clearly than ever, and he points out that, in the United States, Halloween (the former All Hallows' Eve) is no longer the mourning of the ancestors of the parents, but a children's celebration. Dundes posits, "The emphasis is upon the child, the future, rather than upon the deceased ancestors, the past."[3]

A Syntax of Mourning: The Globalization of Grief

Nearly all the newly emerging rituals related to memorialization follow a particular language of mourning, which in turn follows a particular framework that is defined by the ritual, rather than being delineated or limited by culture. Ghostbikes, for example, are universally painted white and installed in a traffic intersection where a biker died, whether in Chicago, São Paulo, Singapore, or Cyprus. Tattoos are limited by the canvas of the body, the tattoo artist's ability, and, most important, the audience's recognition of tattoos as memorials. Tattoo artists, who believe their work to be individual, unique, and a true art form, are in tension with the person seeking to memorialize, who often has the desire to receive a memorial that will be recognizable as such, whereas the tattoo artist seeks to ink a design that is inimitable and highly personal. Similarly, social network memorials operate within end-user constraints developed by software programs, which force social network users globally to memorialize in very similar ways, regardless of cultural or linguistic backgrounds. The Internet is the one type of memorialization that seems to be universal and, interestingly enough, is governed by its own syntax and grammar for memorializing of the dead. The various types of memorialization, as they are becoming more globally recognized and used, are unique because they are limited not by cultural and linguistic constraints, but rather by the constraints of each particular medium. In this way, even memorialization is experiencing a kind of McDonaldization, as new traditions of memorialization subscribe to a universal syntax of remembrance of the dead.

Democratizing Grief

Another commonality is the democratizing effect of popular memorializing, as these memorials give a voice to marginal grievers—those who are not given a place in society to grieve, either because of their social position or because the type of loss they have experienced is considered taboo or is not publicly sanctioned. This democratization of grief has both positive and negative consequences. The network of mourners for a person who dies is often extensive, but the limits and hierarchy placed by both society and the workplace on who can mourn a death are rather rigid. These memorials allow anyone to grieve—even those who did not know the deceased. They offer a popular response not bound by traditional notions of who is allowed to grieve and for whom, as they sidestep the restrictions placed by both the workplace and society. They also allow those who may not traditionally attend the funeral the space to grieve in a public and safe forum. For example, my graduate assistant said that if her neighbor died, she would not feel comfortable going to the funeral, but she would probably leave a note on his Facebook page.[4] She doesn't feel close enough to mourn with the family at a funeral, but she could mourn with the circle of acquaintances on her neighbor's Facebook page. This distinction is important, as these memorials allow the network of grievers to expand beyond traditionally defined social circles. The number of people who have signed on to become members of the Sandy Hook Elementary School memorial Facebook pages (hundreds of thousands on numerous sites) and the RIP Krystle Campbell site (now at 76,000) obviously far exceed the numbers within the social circles of the deceased. Social network memorials reveal a desire and a need by people to mourn these deaths, even if it is within an anonymous community and by people who never knew or met the deceased but somehow feel as though they share in the experience of grieving. This is also borne out at the sites of material memorials, by people such as Greg Zanis, discussed in chapter 1. Zanis's desire and eagerness to participate and build the material memorials at various shooting sites reveal the need of some to be a part of ongoing memorialization, even though they have no personal connection to many of the dead. The negative aspects of the democratization of mourning can be found in the example I gave in chapter 4 of the widow who felt usurped in her position as primary griever; she wanted to be recognized as such but felt her own mourning was eclipsed by the mourning taking place on her dead husband's Facebook page.

Mostly, though, the democratizing role that these forms of memorialization give to the bereaved offers a way of remembering and thinking about the dead that challenges contemporary society's disappearing of both death and bereavement. These democratizing effects can best be described as a form of *communitas,* a term that Victor Turner used to describe an unstructured community in which people are more or less equal.[5] Bobby Alexander discusses the role of Turner's *communitas* in challenging traditional structures: "While social structure is both positive and necessary for social life because it organizes society to meet material needs, it is also problematic. . . . Differentiations among social status and roles, by nature, creates 'alienation.' . . . The primary motivation behind [communitas] . . . is the desire to break free temporarily of social structure in order to transcend its existential limitations and reconfigure it along communitarian lines."[6] Social structures in these new forms of memorialization are much less rigid, and participants in these various forms of bereavement seem to bear this out.[7] Online grieving and participation in chat rooms is not limited to those in the traditional bereavement circle; it extends far beyond that to the traditionally marginalized grievers and even further, to strangers. In their growing popularity, these new forms of memorialization may also reflect the limits of funerary and religious discourse in the bereavement process. Perhaps these types of memorials are growing in popularity partly because they offer (limited) publicly sanctioned forms of thinking about and grieving the dead when the world no longer condones such public expressions of grief.

At the heart of all these forms of memorialization is the desire for grievers to experience a sense of community; these forms of memorialization are all private expressions of mourning exhibited within a public sphere. Grievers are not merely memorializing; they are memorializing for spectators. Victor Turner's use of communitas is apt here, as these memorials—the people who construct them, participate in them, and regularly return to them—are attempting to come to terms with individual loss in a very public way.[8] Visiting a grief chat room, a social network memorial, having a car-decal memorial on one's car, or even stopping by a material memorial is, in some ways, similar to the experience of doing one's work in a coffee shop. Technically, one is not alone—one is surrounded by the people scattered throughout the shop, sipping lattes, chatting with friends, and working on laptop computers—but neither is one actually expected to interact with any of these people. It is a sort of liminal experience of community—perhaps not deeply meaningful, but an attempt nonetheless. One feels, for a moment, that one is not alone in the world. All these memorials demonstrate the need for communitas when confronting death, and the sheer volume of memorials, both material and virtual, demonstrate that they must, on some level, be answering that need.

Memorialization as Identity

In a time when life expectancies are longer than ever, the expression of grief is ironically marginalized. Elizabeth Hallam and Jenny Hockey discuss the social expectations of grief: "Both an impassive face and noisy sobbing are inappropriate. Instead a performance of grief bridges the differentiated spheres of public and private emotionality."[9] The current rituals of grief are extremely restrictive—in expression, in social actors (who can perform them), and in time (through limits placed on how long one can grieve). Rituals of self-identification, and the public setting apart of oneself as mourner, have been lost in today's corporate and global culture. Memorialization still allows remnants of these practices to occur; the tattooing in memory of the deceased, or the car-decal memorial, or even the changing of one's profile photo to one with the deceased is a virtual self-identification as a mourner. Leaving mementos at material memorials for the deceased and writing on Internet memorials also allow traditionally marginalized grievers (friends, exes, and others) to play a role in the grieving process while claiming status as mourner in a virtual world where their grief might be acknowledged.

A Theology of Presence

What these new forms of memorialization lack, however, is the deep, sustained connection of presence, as there is no substitution for the body, no matter how we try. It is, in some ways, a theological issue—the dead have gone missing, and the attempt to fill that absence with narratives, objects, and virtual conversations with strangers can sometimes lead to odd appropriations of the living or bodies that seem grotesque or out of place. Social network memorials, QR codes on tombstones, and virtual avatars are, as Derrida asserted, ghosts from the past haunting the present through technology. Part of the problem is also the idea that bodies can be substituted—that ultimately body parts can be replaced through organ donation, or replicated through steel and plastic. The body—the person—is absent, and in the end that absence must be acknowledged. As Baudrillard writes, "The body as instituted by modern mythology is no more material than the soul. Like the soul, it is an *idea,* or rather—since the term 'idea' does not mean much—it is a hypostatized part-object, a double-privileged and invested as such. It has become, as the soul was in its time, the priveleged substrate of objectivization—*the guiding myth of an ethic of consumption.*"[10]

Disappearing the body as it is dying, and after, when it is dead, is more than a denial of death; it is a denial of the body—the self—and life. Embalming, cremating, moving cemeteries out of the cities, creating narratives of lives, and removing memorials from the public sphere only lead to the personal appropriation of death and the dead—on our bodies, on our belongings (cars and T-shirts), and in our virtual other worlds. Through our unconscious desires or not, dead bodies have disappeared from the landscape of the living, and, ironically, we cannot live without them. Memorialization, then, can be seen as an attempt to reinsert the dead among the living through remembrance.

A Tale of Two Memorials: Boston and West, Texas

As I was finishing this book, the factory explosion in West, Texas, occurred, causing the deaths of fourteen people, including the town's entire volunteer fire department, injuries to more than one hundred people, and heavy damage to several hundred homes. The explosion in West was eclipsed by the Boston Marathon bombings and their aftermath, but the responses to the two explosions and the subsequent memorialization were also very different. The Boston explosions were a deliberate act by two persons (in some ways like the bombing in Oklahoma City years earlier), and they occurred at the site of a crowded event where there was mass media coverage. The West explosion, on the other hand, was largely accidental (though there is some speculation that it might have been arson) and affected an entire town in a rural area of central Texas, and there was little media exposure. West accrued more fatalities, including deaths of first responders that deeply affected the community, but the primary differences were the community's response and subesequent media coverage. In West, streets were immediately shut down, and only residents and first responders were allowed into the affected areas.

Even several months later, the majority of streets were blocked off, and it was difficult even for the media to gain access to the town. Boston, on the other hand, cordoned off several streets and used the media to help track down the bombers, essentially shutting down the city and employing extensive media coverage until one perpetrator was killed and the other caught days later in nearby Watertown. The Internet response to events in Boston was immediate: websites opened for each of the Boston marathon fatalities immediately, and the number of hits multiplied rapidly, reaching the 100,000 mark on many of the sites within days. In contrast, there were minimal Internet responses to the events in West, beyond a hotline through the local newspaper offering donations, housing, and water for those in need, and a small Facebook search page for those whose animals had been lost in the explosion (which had 1,200 members—more, sadly, than the search and rescue page for people in West). In other words, the Internet response to Boston was mainly for spectators who wished to share their ideas, thoughts, and feelings about the events, whereas in West, the Internet response was limited primarily to the immediate needs of West's citizens and their families.

Memorialization has also followed similar lines: the Boston Marathon memorial drew thousands of contributions, including flowers, notes, balloons, and many, many shoes, whereas in West there has been very little memorialization for those who died, beyond flowers left at the fire station and a few signs scattered throughout the town. In Boston both material and virtual memorialization has been prolific; in West, where there were more casualties, material and virtual memorialization is minimal. The difference between the two events in some ways reflects Baudrillard's theory of the saturation of simulacra—that we have begun to remember that which we are told to remember—by the media and others in society. The events in West have left the entire town devastated—without a fire department, a school and nursing home obliterated, and many homes damaged beyond repair—yet Internet memorialization has for the most part neglected it. Another difference (and this cannot be overlooked) is that the town of West is largely Czech (it is known as the Czech heritage capital of Texas), and 85 percent of its 2,800 residents are actively Roman Catholic. The Catholic church, with its heavy emphasis on religious memorialization, may in part be responsible for the fact that those in West have not sought to memorialize in an external and public fashion: perhaps they have not needed to do so. The memorialization of West has been mostly internal, participated in by those in the West community. (President Obama did come to a major service held for those who died, but this event was held not at West but at Baylor University in Waco, twenty minutes down the road.) On the other hand, the memorialization of the Boston bombings has largely occurred in the public eye and the media. President Obama recognized both tragedies, and both services were broadcast on television, but the difference in how these two tradgedies have been remembered and memorialized reveals deeper issues. The citizens of West have a strong communal base to depend on through their mourning; it is a small country town whose residents rely on a Catholic worldview to

Memorialization in West, Texas, has been very limited, as the town is small, the community is tightly knit, and outsiders have largely been kept out. The one form of memorialization that has emerged is these stars, which have appeared all over the community—on street signs, trees, fences—offering sentiments of support and remembrance. Photo by the author

(*Above*) The devastation in West was enormous: hundreds of homes, a school, and a nursing home were destroyed in the blast. Photo by the author (*Below*) Both Boston and West used similar recovery slogans in their memorializations: "West Is Strong" and "Boston Strong" became the rallying cries of unity and support following the explosions in the two cities. Photo by the author

help them with their mourning and grief. The citizens of Boston have had to cobble together a recognizable system of grief and remembrance through the Boston Marathon memorial and Internet chat rooms, depending largely on a secular and popular mourning discourse in the public eye. West and Boston, and all grassroots memorialization, reflect the tensions at work in our culture: the personal struggle to mediate reality in a world that disguises it, and a desire to make meaning of death in a world that denies it. Unless we can resurrect death itself from its banishment in the contemporary world, memorialization will continue so that the dead can remain in the world of the living.

Acknowledgments

There are many people who helped see this project to its completion, and so I thank, in no particular order, everyone who supported and encouraged me in my research, ideas, and writing. First, I thank Ashley Runyon and all the editorial staff at the University Press of Kentucky for taking on this project. Thanks also go to Carey Newman, director of Baylor University Press, who gave me much encouragement and the confidence to move forward with this book, and who particularly helped me see that it was a valuable enterprise. I am deeply grateful to Baylor University, the Honors College, the Baylor Interdisciplinary Core, and the Religion Department for giving me financial support for the project, granting me a summer sabbatical in which to conduct my research and graduate assistants to help with my scholarship. I am indebted to both Tom Hibbs and Anne-Marie Schultz for their support throughout this process. I am appreciative of the invaluable assistance I received from Lacy Crocker, Anna Beal, Susan Moudry, and David Wilmington, all of whom were partners at one time or another in the creative process of developing this manuscript, and who gave me much needed assistance in perfecting and editing the manuscript in its various stages, and to Jim Nogalski, who directed their assistance my way. I am grateful for my group of women colleagues here at Baylor— Brooke Blevins, Greta Buehrle, Natalie Carnes, and Kristen Pond—who make life a little easier and full of laughter. Finally, I thank Jim West, Susan Lum, Gailynn Williamson, Joe Chernisky, George Tanabe, Rob Weller, and Kimberley Patton for their mentoring and support over the years. Their feedback, encouragement, and hugs have made it wonderful to be on this path, and it is because of them that I am where I am today.

No project like this would be complete without the support of friends and family, and it is to them that I owe the most appreciation for keeping me sane and sharing their company. To my family I owe much gratitude for all their love, help with child care, and companionship. Dad and Joyce, thank you for the tea parties, for listening, and for helping me have fun when I have been stressed. You are great grandparents. Martha, thank you for being a great second mother and a wonderful grandmother to Maia. Lynn, I am so glad you are my sister and Maia's auntie. Kehaulani, your friendship has been one of life's finest rewards, and seeing Kahi being born after watching my mother die is one of the greatest gifts you have given me: the knowledge that even in the midst of death, life goes on. Lily, thank you for being in our lives—you have brought us joy, wisdom, and fun and helped me see how important it is to embrace life in the midst of pain. I am a deep admirer of yours. Karen, Sam, Nathan, and Jessie, many thanks for hosting us year after year in paradise. We have enjoyed your company, and I have savored your wisdom and humor. Charity, Josh, John, Dawn, Katie, Kyle, Emmanuelle, Tenzin, Julie, Diane, Alden, Mike, Christy, Harvey, Ronnie, Blake, Michele, Kevin, Abby, Tom, Carlos, Jen, and Paul, thank you for your friendship and your support; I am so grateful for your continued companionship on this journey of life. Last, thanks to Maia, my beautiful daughter, who makes me stop and see the absolutely stunning beauty in this fragile world. I love you.

Interview Questions for Tattoo Artists

Have you ever done memorial tattoos in your shop?

What percentage of tattoos do you think are memorial tattoos?

Has the number of memorial tattoos you have done increased in the last five years? Ten years? Since your practice has been open?

Why do you think this is the case?

Do you do tattoos with cremains? Why or why not? Have you received a request to do this?

What kind of memorial tattoos have you done? Can you share your pictures with me?

Are they different for men and women? If so, how?

Who are the memorials generally for?

Why do you think people get these memorial tattoos?

Interview Questions for Car-Decal Memorial Manufacturers

How many memorial decals do you produce per month or year?

Has this number gone up in recent years?

Are there particular geographical areas that order more of these?

Are the majority in English or Spanish?

Who are the majority of these memorials for (young people or old people)?

Can you send me some examples of more popular car-decal memorials? What kinds of designs are most often requested?

Do you have a memorial decal that was particularly beautiful or difficult to design?

How many are usually ordered at one time? Are they single orders or bulk orders?

When the company was founded, did you see memorial decals as a future part of the business? Why or why not?

Notes

The quotations in the epigraph were taken from the following sources: Jean Baudrillard, *Simulacra and Simulation,* trans. Sheila Faria Glaser (Ann Arbor: University of Michigan Press, 1994), 6. Jacques Derrida, in *Ghost Dance,* a 1983 film by Ken McMullen (London: Mediabox Limited, 2008).

Introduction

1. James W. Green, "The Future of Death: Three Scenarios of Changing Metaphors and Changing Practices," talk given at Columbia University seminar on death, "Journey to the End—Death, Dying and Bereavement in 21st Century America," March 24, 2012. In this talk Green pointed out that when dying patients are in the hospital, their family and friends become "visitors," and it is doctors and nurses who deem themselves most essential to the well-being of the sick, essentially turning the traditional model of family and the social structures we live in upside down.

2. Refrigerated cars allowed for the transport not only of corpses, but also of meat, transforming grocery transportation and distribution to the management of corpses and death.

3. Philippe Ariès, *The Hour of Our Death,* trans. Helen Weaver (New York: Knopf, 1981); Philippe Ariès, *Western Attitudes toward Death: From the Middle Ages to the Present,* trans. Patricia M. Ranum (Baltimore: Johns Hopkins University Press, 1974).

4. Whole-brain death (as opposed to partial-brain death, which is the definition generally accepted in the United Kingdom) is the definition of death accepted by both the American Medical Association and the American Bar Association and is currently the accepted understanding of death in forty-six states, thirty-six of which have adopted the Uniform Determination of Death Act's definition. This definition accepts death based on three criteria: (1) severe coma, (2) absent brainstem reflexes, or (3) sustained apnea (or a combination thereof). This definition of brain death often requires more costly health care and sustaining the body beyond normal parameters, partly because it benefits the harvesting of organs for donation to others. The cost of sustaining artificial respiration and feeding of the body, however, is most often borne by the family of the soon-to-be-deceased. In contrast, in the United Kingdom, where public rather than private health care is responsible for the costs of keeping the body alive, death is defined as only partial-brain

death or brainstem death. B. Brody and A. Halevy, "Brain Death: Reconciling Definitions, Criteria, and Tests," *Annals of Internal Medicine* 119, no. 6 (1993): 519–525; F. Plum, "Clinical Standards and Technological Confirmatory Tests in Diagnosing Brain Death," in *The Definition of Death: Contemporary Controversies,* ed. S. J. Younger, R. M. Arnold, and R. Schapiro (Baltimore: Johns Hopkins University Press, 1999), 34–65.

5. Three and four days are numbers that signify completeness and abundance in Western culture, and the number three has particular significance in the United States. Alan Dundes discusses the importance of the number three in his work "The Number Three in American Culture," in Dundes, *Every Man His Way: Readings in Cultural Anthropology* (Englewood Cliffs, N.J.: Prentice-Hall, 1968), 401–424.

6. Lisa Guerin, *Employment Law: The Essential HR Desk Reference* (Berkeley, Calif.: Nolo, 2011).

7. See Richard Block, "Work-Family Legislation in the United States, Canada, and Western Europe: A Quantitative Comparison," *Pepperdine Law Review* 34, no. 2 (2007): 11, for an excellent analysis and quantitative breakdown by country, and for the United States and Canada, each state and province's policy on all types of employment leave, including bereavement leave.

8. Christopher Hunter, Louisa Lam, and Ketong Lin, *Employment Law in China,* 2nd ed. (Hong Kong: CCH Hong Kong Limited, 2008), 120–121.

9. Terrie Lloyd, "Terrie's Job Tips," www.daijob.com/en/columns/terrie/article/334 (accessed November 19, 2013).

10. Philip M. Berkowitz, Thomas Müller-Bonanni, and Anders Etgen Reitz, *International Labor and Employment Law: Labor and Employment Law in Argentina* (Chicago: American Bar Association, 2006), 79.

11. Colombia's Political Constitution of 1991 dictates current labor laws: "Invest in Colombia," www.investincolombia.com.co/Adjuntos/103_Chapter%204%20Labor%20Framework.pdf (accessed January 1, 2014).

12. For a full list of relationships and their definitions covered by the bereavement policies for U.S. government employees, see the following website: Office of Personnel Management, U.S. Government, "Fact Sheet: Definitions Related to Family Member and Immediate Relative for Purposes of Sick Leave, Funeral Leave, Voluntary Leave Transfer, Voluntary Leave Bank, and Emergency Leave Transfer," www.opm.gov/policy-data-oversight/pay-leave/leave-administration/fact-sheets/definitions-related-to-family-member-and-immediate-relative-for-purposes-of-sick-leave/ (accessed November 19, 2013).

13. Disney Bereavement Leave Policy, Disney Corporation.

14. Ibid.

15. Ibid.

16. Hourly employees are given twenty-four hours of bereavement leave, but this equals the salaried employees' leave, if calculated at eight hours per working day. AOL Bereavement Leave Policy, America Online, New York.

17. Walmart employee, interview by Candi Cann, audio recording (Walmart, Waco, Tex., May 6, 2013).

18. The APA maintains a website for the *DSM 5*, "DSM 5," www.dsm5. org/Pages/Default.aspx (accessed November 29, 2013).

19. This reclassification is complex and finely nuanced. The reclassification of grief *without* the bereavement exclusion does allow for the quicker treatment of depression associated with grief, and this is a positive result. That being said, however, the two-week window on diagnosing depressive symptoms is rather narrow and has received the most criticism, particularly when traumatic death is involved. The exclusion would be more beneficial if the time frame were wider.

20. The effect of death and the losses associated with it can be somewhat measured through the fact that one's earliest childhood memories generally include that of the first death experience, whether human or animal. For more on this, see JoNell A. Usher and Ulric Neisser, "Childhood Amnesia and the Beginnings of Memory for Four Early Life Events," *Journal of Experimental Psychology: General* 122, no. 2 (1993): 155.

21. Carol Smart, *Personal Life* (Cambridge, U.K.: Polity, 2007), and Glenys Caswell, "Personalisation in Scottish Funerals: Individualised Ritual or Relational Process?" *Mortality* 16, no. 3 (2011): 248–249.

22. J. R. Averill and E. P. Nunley, "Grief as an Emotion and as a Disease: A Social-Constructionist Perspective," in *Handbook of Bereavement: Theory, Research, and Intervention*, ed. Margaret S. Stroebe, Wolfgang Stroebe, and Robert O. Hansson (New York: Cambridge University Press, 1993), 82.

23. For more on disenfranchised grief, see Kenneth J. Doka, ed., *Disenfranchised Grief* (Lexington, Mass.: Lexington Books/D. C. Heath, 1989).

24. C. A. Haney, C. Leimer, and J. Lowery, "Spontaneous Memorialization: Violent Death and Emerging Mourning Ritual," *Omega* 35, no. 2 (1997): 159–171.

25. Jennifer Clark and Majella Franzmann, "Authority from Grief, Presence and Place in the Making of Roadside Memorials," *Death Studies* 30, no. 6 (2006): 581.

26. Maurice Merleau-Ponty, *Phenomenology of Perception*, trans. Colin Smith (London: Routledge, 1962), 162.

1. The Bodiless Memorial

1. Jack Santino uses the term *spontaneous memorialization* in his book *Spontaneous Shrines and the Public Memorialization of Death* (New York: Palgrave Macmillan, 2006) (and before that in a 1999 article describing murals to fallen gang members), an edited collection of essays about memorials that emerge at the grassroots level in popular culture. This term is most often used to describe memorials for victims of traumatic death. Though I use this

term interchangeably with *grassroots memorialization,* I am a bit wary of it, as I think it implies, on some levels, that these memorials themselves emerge without agency or an intentional or collective effort, which I believe the brief notes on Greg Zanis somewhat contradict (see the end of this chapter). *Grassroots memorialization* more aptly describes the phenomenon we see emerging at the popular level, and there is a good discussion on this in Peter Jan Margry and Cristina Sánchez-Carretero, eds., *Grassroots Memorials: The Politics of Memorializing Traumatic Death* (New York: Berghahn Books, 2011).

2. The World Trade Center (WTC) site first started as a popular memorial, as people memorialized at a grassroots level, and then it was appropriated by the U.S. government as an official memorial. In this way the WTC memorial functions on two levels—at the popular grassroots level, and from the top down as a government-sponsored memorial to help spread its own message of nationalism and its foreign affairs agenda.

3. Erika Doss, *Memorial Mania: Public Feeling in America* (Chicago: University of Chicago Press, 2010).

4. For more on the role of the wake or viewing in the grief process, see George L. Engel, "Grief and Grieving," *AJN: American Journal of Nursing* 64, no. 9 (1964): 93–98.

5. Karen Wilson Baptist, "Diaspora: Death without a Landscape," *Mortality* 15, no. 4 (2010): 296.

6. Clark and Franzmann, "Authority from Grief," 593.

7. Craig Young and Duncan Light, "Corpses, Dead Body Politics and Agency in Human Geography: Following the Corpse of Dr. Petru Groza," *Transactions of the Institute of British Geographers* 38, no. 1 (2013): 135–148.

8. Avril Maddrell and James D. Sidaway, eds., *Deathscapes: Spaces for Death, Dying, Mourning and Remembrance* (Burlington, Vt.: Ashgate, 2010).

9. For more on this, see Frederic Wakeman, "Revolutionary Rites: The Remains of Chiang Kai-shek and Mao Tse-tung," *Representations* 10 (Spring 1985): 146–193.

10. Barnes discusses the kidnapping, disappearance, and reappearance in his biography *Evita, First Lady: A Biography of Eva Peron* (New York: Grove Press, 1978).

11. President Obama clearly recognized the danger of retaining the corpse of Osama bin Laden after bin Laden's capture and assassination. For this reason, bin Laden's body was disposed of at sea, preventing a cult of his corpse, but this then created a problem for the American public, who demanded proof that he was in fact dead. The importance of this disposal of the body cannot be understated, because Obama recognized the potential agency of bin Laden's corpse to create reverence and solidarity among militant Muslims, but also to create animosity among American who might seek retaliation for the events of 9/11 by defiling the corpse.

12. For more on this, see Young and Light, "Corpses."

13. Robert Pogue Harrison, *The Dominion of the Dead* (Chicago: University of Chicago Press, 2003), 147–148.

14. Young and Light, "Corpses."

15. Baptist, "Diaspora," 304.

16. Clark and Franzmann, "Authority from Grief," 591. They go on to write, "It appears that for many grieving families and friends the roadside memorial may be of greater significance than the cemetery or crematorium space where bodies or ashes reside. Perhaps this is so because burial customs have gradually lost some of their spiritual dimension and attachment to place. Before the nineteenth century the place to be buried was the churchyard within the precinct of hallowed ground, with other believers of like faith. A stranger could not be buried there, nor one who committed suicide, indicating the authority of the church over demographic and theological matters. The modern cemetery developed as an alternative burial place to accommodate those who could not meet the residency and theological requirements of the church. It was a democratized and secularized place even though, in some cases, it was divided into sections for Christian denominations or other religions. In the age of liberal capitalism anyone could ensure their burial, as a commodity to be bought, not a favor to be earned. The cemetery is a civil space, open to all, regardless of belief or unbelief. Thomas Laqueur argues that it does not 'speak of a place but of people from all places . . . unknown to each other in life and thrown together in a place with which they might have had only the most transitory acquaintance.'" Clark and Franzmann "Authority from Grief," 592.

17. H. F. Senie, "Mourning in Protest: Spontaneous Memorial and the Sacralization of Public Space," in Santino, *Spontaneous Shrines*, 41–56, observes, "It may be precisely because cemeteries and the function they once served have receded from civic consciousness that the practice of spontaneous memorials has flourished" (45).

18. Baptist, "Diaspora," 294–307. See also Grey Gundaker, "At Home on the Other Side: African American Burials as Commemorative Landscapes," in *Places of Commemoration: Search for Identity and Landscape Design*, ed. J. Wolschke-Bulmahn (Washington, D.C.: Dumbarton Oaks, 2001), 46.

19. Baptist, "Diaspora," 300.

20. Clark and Franzmann, "Authority from Grief," 587, write, "Memorials may appear to be a popular expression in contradiction to the expectations of organized authority, but this does not mean they have complete communal endorsement. Public space may be regulated by the state but it is for the use of the wider community. . . . The roadside is public, secular space, but memorial builders assume the authority to transfer this space into a sacred place. An empowering agent may be their own sense of spirituality informed by an eclectic knowledge of religion but not necessarily dictated by the practice or ideas of any one religion or denomination."

21. There has, however, been memorialization of those hurt and killed in the Aum Shinrikyo subway attacks, but these memorializations have been organized and carried out mostly by government and transportation officials. For more on this, see Cherrie Lou Billones, "18th Anniversary of Aum Shinrikyo Subway Gas Attack Remembered in Tokyo," *Japan Daily Press,* March 20, 2013, http://japandailypress.com/18th-anniversary-of-aum-shinrikyo-subway-gas-attack-remembered-in-tokyo-2025515 (accessed May 8, 2013).

22. For more on Chinese American funeral customs, see Linda Sun Crowder, "Chinese Funerals in San Francisco Chinatown: American Chinese Expressions in Mortuary Ritual Performance," *Journal of American Folklore* 113, no. 450 (2000): 451–463. She describes how Chinese American funerals in San Francisco's Chinatown encapsulate aspects of both the Chinese diaspora and American funeral customs (such as the elimination of walking barefoot after the corpse in favor of riding in a hearse, or even the hiring of an American-sounding funeral band.

23. Though part of the interaction between the realms of the living and the dead in Japan and China, deaths of babies and children are not treated in a positive manner, because they are viewed as ominous. Because of this, the interaction of dead children with the living world is seen as negative, and the living then must find ways to placate their spirits. In Japan elaborate Buddhist grieving rituals, known as *mizuko kuyo,* have been put in place for grieving over aborted fetuses, because it is believed that they will return to haunt the living. In China, before the Communist revolution of 1949, children traditionally were not even given an official name until they reached the age of five or began their schooling. Until that time, they were given a "milkname" or a nickname, ancestor tablets were given only to adults—men of the family, and women who had borne sons and thus continued the family lineage and demonstrated their role in the reciprocal roles of filial piety. For more on *mizuko kuyo,* see William R. LaFleur, *Liquid Life: Abortion and Buddhism in Japan* (Princeton: Princeton University Press, 1992). For more on death in China, see James Lee Watson and Evelyn S. Rawski, eds., *Death Ritual in Late Imperial and Modern China* (Berkeley: University of California Press, 1988).

24. The Madres de la Plaza de Mayo in Argentina used the absence of the corpse as a way to garner political agency and protest the disappearance of their children. In some ways, this was an inversion of the standard formula, for it was the very absence, tied to their presence as mothers, that made the imagined presence of the corpses so strong. For more on the Madres and their role in recovering the disappeared in the Dirty War of Argentina, see Marysa Navarro, "The Personal Is Political: Las Madres de Plaza de Mayo," in *Power and Popular Protest: Latin American Social Movements,* ed. Susan Eckstein (Berkeley: University of California Press, 1989), 241–258.

25. Timothy Shortell, "Radicalization of Religious Discourse in El Salva-

dor: The Case of Oscar A. Romero," *Sociology of Religion* 62, no. 1 (2001): 87–103.

26. The latest example involved the execution and mutilation of forty-nine people who were then dumped in the middle of Mexico's northern highway leading to Texas. Executions and mass body dumpings have become the primary method of protest over transport routes between the two major drug cartels, the Zeta and Sinaloa. Corpses here function as a way to intimidate and pressure the government and the Mexican public in a powerful display of brutal force enacted through not only the execution of bodies, but the mutilation of corpses.

27. See Stanley Brandes, "Sugar, Colonialism, and Death: On the Origins of Mexico's Day of the Dead," *Comparative Studies in Society and History* 39, no. 2 (1997): 270–299.

28. See Daniel H. Levine, "The Future of Christianity in Latin America," *Journal of Latin American Studies* 41, no. 1 (2009): 121–145.

29. Robert A. Orsi, *Between Heaven and Earth: The Religious Worlds People Make and the Scholars Who Study Them* (Princeton: Princeton University Press, 2005), 101.

30. Uruguay statistics are from Instituto Nacional de Estadística, "Cencos 2011," www.ine.gub.uy (accessed March 11, 2013).

31. See Candi K. Cann, "Holy Wars, Cold Wars and Dirty Wars: Manufacturing Martyrs in the Two-thirds World: A Case Study" (Ph.D. diss., Harvard University, 2009).

32. Max Weber, *The Protestant Ethic and the Spirit of Capitalism*, trans. Talcott Parsons (1930; repr., London: Routledge, 1992).

33. "Ghostbikes: How To," http://ghostbikes.org/howto (accessed November 20, 2013).

34. Interestingly enough, when Van Der Tuin started, he used some of the mangled remains of real bikes in his memorialization, but these are no longer used.

35. Robert Dobler argues that in addition to expressing grief in a public sphere, ghostbikes redefine public spaces as significant and contested spaces. See Robert Thomas Dobler, "Ghost Bikes," in Margry and Sánchez-Carretero, *Grassroots Memorials,* 169–187.

36. Clark and Franzmann, "Authority from Grief," 594.

37. See ibid., 579–599, in which the authors claim that memorial creators make secular spaces sacred, and public spaces private, through the act of memorialization.

38. Sylvia Grider, "Memorializing Shooters with Their Victims," in Margry and Sánchez-Carretero, *Grassroots Memorials,* 114–120.

39. Prescott Carlson, "The Man behind the Crosses," *Miscellaneous,* February 17, 2008, accessed March 16, 2013, http://chicagoist.com/2008/02/17/whos_leaving_th.php (accessed March 16, 2013).

40. It should also be noted that in addition to his crosses, Zanis likes to

make paintings of the communities receiving his crosses; the paintings depict both the crosses and the people receiving the crosses. Thus, his "art" is two-fold, comprising the performative aspect and the recounting in a painting of that performative element.

41. Kurtis Lee, "Makeshift Memorial to Aurora Theater Shooting Victims Removed," *Denver Post*, September 20, 2012, www.denverpost.com/breakingnews/ci_21591061/aurora-removes-memorial-at-theater-shooting-site (accessed March 11, 2013).

42. The Aurora History Museum can be found at www.auroragov.org/ThingsToDo/ArtsandCulture/AuroraHistoryMuseum/index.htm, though as of March 2013, no memorial objects have been catalogued or uploaded to a database. Part of the memorial will live on virtually at http://gigapan.com/gigapans/110384 and http://gigapan.com/gigapans/110385. The city will continue to provide access to the items at a secured location, provided by what the city calls a "community partner." The white crosses that stood at the memorial across from the theater will be delivered to the families or stored by the city, depending on the family's preference. The Aurora History Museum will handle the archiving of items not collected by families. The public will be able to view a display of condolences and banners not taken by family members at the Aurora Municipal Center, 15151 E. Alameda Parkway; see Sarah Castellanos, "City Removes Items from Temporary Aurora Theater Shooting Memorial," *Aurora Sentinel*, September 20, 2012, www.aurorasentinel.com/news/metroaurora/removal/ (accessed November 20, 2013).

43. As of March 2013, several of the families are suing Cinemark theaters, for what they believe to be a lack of security at the theater. Cinemark employees have been instructed not to discuss the case publicly.

44. Clayton Sandell, "Aurora Shooting Victims' Families Outraged by Invitation to Reopening," *ABC News*, January 2, 2013, http://abcnews.go.com/blogs/headlines/2013/01/aurora-shooting-victims-families-outraged-by-invitation-to-reopening/ (accessed March 12, 2013).

45. Melanie Asmar, "Aurora Century Theater Reopens Six Months after Shootings with Speeches, *The Hobbit*," *Denver Westword*, January 18, 2013, http://blogs.westword.com/latestword/2013/01/aurora_century_theater_reopens_the_hobbit_photos.php (accessed March 18, 2013).

46. Sylvia Grider also discusses the relationship between intentionality and "spontaneous memorialization" in "Public Grief and the Politics of Memorial: Contesting the Memory of 'the Shooters' at Columbine High School," *Anthropology Today* 23, no. 3 (2007): 3–7.

47. Donald Kraybill, "Amish Memorials: The Nickel Mines Pasture and Quiet Forgiveness," *Huffington Post*, September 30, 2011, www.huffingtonpost.com/donald-kraybill/amish-memorials-the-nickel-mines-memorial_b_982144.html (accessed March 18, 2013).

48. Though some might argue that the trees operate as living memorials

of the lives lost, there is no constructed memorial, nor is there signage to explain the tree memorial; rather, only those living there (and those who have read about the trees and their placement) understand the meaning behind the trees and know their location.

49. Brad Igou, "Amish Country News," www.amishnews.com/amisharticles/religioustraditions.htm#Part%20Six:%20The%20Funeral%20Service (accessed March 15, 2013).

50. Barack Obama, "Remarks on the Shootings in Newtown, Connecticut," *Daily Compilation of Presidential Documents,* December 14, 2012.

51. "Conn. Governor: 'Evil Visited This Community,'" Associated Press, December 14, 2012, http://on.aol.com/video/conn--governor--evil-visited-this-community-517599663 (accessed March 21, 2013).

52. As he did after the other shootings, Zanis made the crosses in his workshop and personally delivered them to Newtown. And as he had in Aurora, he made crosses only for those who were killed—twenty-six crosses in all. Zanis didn't make crosses for either the killer or his mother, claiming, "This guy goes straight to hell and burns for eternity," referring to Lanza. "And I believe he is getting his just punishment." William Marsden, "In Newtown, White Crosses, Tidy Lawns and Teddy Bears for Sale," *Windsor (Ont.) Star,* December 16, 2012, http://o.canada.com/2012/12/16/in-newtown-white-crosses-tidy-lawns-and-teddy-bears-for-sale/ (accessed March 21, 2013).

53. Ray Rivera, "Asking What to Do with Symbols of Grief as Memorials Pile Up," *New York Times,* January 5, 2013, www.nytimes.com/2013/01/06/nyregion/as-memorials-pile-up-newtown-struggles-to-move-on.html?pagewanted=1&_r=0 (accessed March 20, 2013).

54. Ibid.

55. Sara Mosle, "The Lives Unlived in Newtown," *New York Times Magazine,* December 30, 2012, 7.

56. Laura E. Tanner, *Lost Bodies: Inhabiting the Borders of Life and Death* (Ithaca: Cornell University Press, 2006), 13.

2. Wearing the Dead

1. The English word *tattoo* has its origins in Samoa (Micronesia), in the word *tatau,* which was supposedly imported to Samoa from Fiji. Regardless, though the word is relatively new to the English language (from the time of Captain Cook's voyages to Polynesia, where sailors embraced the art of tattooing and brought the practice back to Europe), the art of tattooing has a long history. Tattoo historians speculate that the connection of tattoos with Polynesia allowed tattoos to escape the Western association of tattoos with the derelict and unsavory aspects of society and move them into more exotic territory, associated with the "romantic" otherness of the Pacific island

culture. For more on this, see Jane Caplan, ed., *Written on the Body: The Tattoo in European and American History* (Princeton: Princeton University Press, 2000), xvi.

2. Noah Scheinfeld, "Tattoos and Religion," *Clinics in Dermatology* 25, no. 4 (2007): 362–366.

3. Maarten Hesselt van Dinter, *The World of Tattoo: An Illustrated History* (Amsterdam: KIT, 2005), 30.

4. James Bradley, "Body Commodification? Class and Tattoos in Victorian Britain," in Caplan, *Written on the Body,* 136–155.

5. Mary Kosut, "An Ironic Fad: The Commodification and Consumption of Tattoos," *Journal of Popular Culture* 39, no. 6 (2006): 1035.

6. A. E. Laumann and A. J. Derick, "Tattoos and Body Piercings in the United States: A National Data Set," *Journal of the American Academy of Dermatology* 55, no. 3 (2006): 413–421.

7. Pew Research Center, "Millennials' Judgments about Recent Trends Not So Different," January 7, 2010, http://pewresearch.org/pubs/1455/millennial-generation-technological-communication-advances-societal-change (accessed July 7, 2012).

8. This Chinese classic, also translated as *All Men Are Brothers* or *Outlaws of the Marsh,* is considered one of the great classic novels in Chinese literature and is required reading for anybody growing up in China.

9. Pet tattooing has recently emerged as a popular phenomenon, however, in both China and Vietnam; people give tattooed fish as gifts for good luck. Leon Watson, "Etch-a-Fish Craze Is Condemned," *London Sun,* August 14, 2009, www.thesun.co.uk/sol/homepage/news/2588264/Etch-a-fish-craze-is-condemned.html (accessed May 14, 2012).

10. Feng discusses the use of tattoos in Song Dynasty China, in much the same way as the Romans in Imperial Rome used them as a form of corporal punishment. See W. E. I. Feng, "On the Song Military System: A Case from Tattoo," *Journal of Historical Science* 9 (2005): 8.

11. For more on tattooing among Chinese ethnic minorities, see Y. A. O. Li-juan, "Research on the Tattoo on the Women of Li People in Hainan Province," *Journal of the Central University for Nationalities* 3 (2005): 19, and L. I. U. Jun, "A First Probe into the Tattoo on the Face in Dulong Ethnic Group," *Journal of the Central University for Nationalities (Philosophy and Social Sciences Edition)* 6 (2007): 15.

12. Mieko Yamada, "Westernization and Cultural Resistance in Tattooing Practices in Contemporary Japan," *International Journal of Cultural Studies* 12, no. 4 (2009): 319.

13. Margo DeMello, "Part 46," in DeMello, *Encyclopedia of Body Adornment* (Westport, Conn.: Greenwood, 2007), 213.

14. Betty Fullard-Leo, "Body Art," *Coffee Times,* Spring–Summer 1999, http://coffeetimes.com/tattoos.htm (accessed November 29, 2013). In mod-

ern romanization of Hawaiian, this would read, "He eha ui no, he nui loa la ku'u aloha."

15. Michael D. Coogan, Marc Z. Brettler, Carol Ann Newsom, and Pheme Perkins, eds., *The New Oxford Annotated Bible with the Apocrypha: New Revised Standard Version* (New York: Oxford University Press, 2010), 171.

16. Saul Olyan argues that the reason for this proscription is that tattooing a sign of mourning is permanent, and it prevents one from entering the temple because one is not considered whole. "Unlike other mourning practices that separate and mark the mourner over the dead, the petitioner, and others who embrace mourning, laceration and shaving are not easily reversible. . . . Unlike the majority of mourning rites that can be reversed at will, which last only as long as the mourner remains separated from the community, the physical evidence of laceration and shaving outlast the community attested, seven-day mourning period." After this period, it is argued that the Hebrews moved to more transient expressions of mourning. For more on this, see Saul M. Olyan, *Biblical Mourning: Ritual and Social Dimensions* (New York: Oxford University Press, 2004), 115–116.

17. The Forward and Ron Dicker, "Jews with Tattoos," *Haaretz,* October 11, 2009.

18. Though tattooing is still generally considered taboo in Judaism, restrictions against burial of Jews with tattoos in Jewish cemeteries have relaxed in the last century, perhaps owing more to the expansion of Reform Judaism than to particular attitudes toward tattooing itself. Yair Ettinger, "Son Gets Dad's Auschwitz Tattoo on Own Arm," *Haaretz,* January 5, 2008.

19. Islam is very clear on the prohibition of tattoos: "It is narrated that 'Abd-Allaah ibn Mas'ood (may Allah be pleased with him) said: 'May Allah curse the women who do tattoos and those for whom tattoos are done, those who pluck their eyebrows and those who file their teeth for the purpose of beautification and alter the creation of Allah" (al-Bukhaari, al-Libaas, 5587; Muslim, al-Libaas, 5538). See "Ruling of Tattoos in Islam," www.muslimconverts.com/cosmetics/tattoos.htm (accessed May 15, 2012).

20. These quotes come from www.hadithcollection.com (spelling and grammar as in the originals), and if one is interested in researching the Hadith in depth, this is a good starting point for the English speaker who does not know Arabic. Specifically, the first, "Abu Dawud Book 028, Hadith Number 4157," is at www.hadithcollection.com/abudawud/260-Abu%20Dawud%20Book%2028.%20Combing%20The%20Hair/17960-abu-dawud-book-028-hadith-number-4157.html, and the second, "Sahih Bukhari Volume 003, Book 034, Hadith Number 440," is at www.hadithcollection.com/sahihbukhari/67-Sahih%20Bukhari%20Book%2034.%20Sales%20and%20Trade/2513-sahih-bukhari-volume-003-book-034-hadith-number-440.html (both accessed May 5, 2013).

21. R. Vora, "Inscribe His Name: Tattoos and India's Ramnaami Community," *World and I* 12 (1997): 200–207.

22. Sinfah Tunsarawuth and Todd Pittman, "Thailand Seeks to Ban Buddha Tattoos for Tourists," *Huffington Post*, June 2, 2011, www.huffingtonpost.com/2011/06/02/thailand-buddha-tattoo-ban_n_870336.html (accessed May 15, 2012).

23. Kimberley Matas, "Memorialize the Loss of Loved Ones," *Arizona Republic*, September 9, 2008, www.azcentral.com/arizonarepublic/local/articles/2008/09/09/20080909memorialtattoo0909.html (accessed July 5, 2012).

24. It should be noted, however, that tattoos of footprints and handprints of infants and children are also inked to celebrate the *birth* of a child, and are not used solely for memorializing dead children.

25. Donna G. (alias), interview by Candi Cann, audio recording, Kailua, Hawaii, March 9, 2011.

26. See Norman Brier, "Grief Following Miscarriage: A Comprehensive Review of the Literature," *Journal of Women's Health*, 17, no. 3 (April 2008): 451–464.

27. "Infants Remembered in Silence," www.irisremembers.com/memories/memorialtattoos.cfm (accessed November 22, 2013).

28. "Tattoo Update," http://forums.thebump.com/discussion/12053978/tattoo-update-pip; "Memorial Tattoo Question—Aw Sorry . . . ," http://forums.thebump.com/discussion/12164411/memorial-tattoo-question-aw-sorry (both accessed January 1, 2014).

29. Ibid.

30. Ibid.

31. "Do You Mind Showing Me Your Memorial Tattoo?" Community Forum, The Bump, http://forums.thebump.com/discussion/7764074/do-you-mind-showing-me-your-memorial-tattoo (accessed January 1, 2014); "Tattoo?" Community Forum, The Bump, http://forums.thebump.com/discussion/7542221/tattoo (accessed January 7, 2104); "Tattoo in Memory of Your Baby?" Netmums, http://www.netmums.com/coffeehouse/advice-support-40/miscarriage-stillbirth-loss-child-boards-548/miscarriage-stillbirth-loss-child-49/544555-tattoo-memory-your-baby-all.html (accessed January 7, 2014).

32. Kimberley Matas, "Memorial Tattoos Ease Loss for Family, Friends," *Arizona Daily Star*, August 31, 2008, http://azstarnet.com/news/local/memorial-tattoos-ease-loss-for-family-friends/article_acafd753-a0c9-5c1d-867a-355b34db17a9.html (accessed April 19, 2013).

33. Roger Chartier writes that Louis Marin saw that "a double meaning and a double function are thus assigned to representation: to make an absence present, but also to exhibit its own image as presence, hence to constitute the person who looks at it as the looking subject." Roger Chartier, *On the Edge of the Cliff: History, Language, and Practices,* trans. Lydia G. Cochrane (Baltimore: Johns Hopkins University Press, 1997), 91.

34. For more on this, see Caplan, *Written on the Body.*

35. "Soldiers headed off to war tend to favor vintage, gung-ho Americana. . . . The second type of military tattoo is for soldiers who want to make their uniform permanent. . . . Religious iconography constitutes a third category of military tattoo. . . . A fourth type of military tattoo stands as a reminder of the human cost of . . . war. . . . Memorial tattoos honor friends and comrades who've died in war." Michael May, "The Skins They Carried: Military Tattoos in the Age of Iraq," *Texas Observer,* March 21, 2008, www.texasobserver.org/2722-the-skins-they-carried-military-tattoos-in-the-age-of-iraq/ (accessed May 21, 2012).

36. Ibid.

37. Alliance of Hope for Suicide Survivors, "Memorial Tattoos," www .facebook.com/media/set/?set=a.200381279984035.42812.200329196655910.

38. See "Memorial Stuff" in the drop-down menu under "Tim" at www .withouttim.com.

39. Nathalie-Kyoko Stucky and Jake Adelstein, "In Japan, Tattoos Are Not Just for Yakuza Anymore," *Japan Sub-Culture,* January 2, 2013, www. japansubculture.com/in-japan-tattoos-are-not-just-for-yakuza-anymore/ (accessed May 5, 2013); Justin McCurry, "Mayor of Osaka Launches Crusade against Tattoos," *Guardian,* May 17, 2012, www.theguardian.com/ world/2012/may/17/mayor-osaka-tattoos.

40. Bryce S. Dubee, "Japanese Water Parks Banning People with Tattoos from Entering Premises," *Stars and Stripes,* July 12, 2008, www.stripes.com/ news/japanese-water-parks-banning-people-with-tattoos-from-entering-premises-1.80904 (accessed May 7, 2013).

41. These portrait tattoos, though, might be the shops' specialty, and are not necessarily indicative of a particular form of memorialization that is occurring.

42. Also similar to the memorial card and memorial tattoo is the Latin American ex-voto, an offering to a saint. Ex-votos usually contain three aspects: an illustration of a miraculous event (usually recovery from an illness or the resolution of a difficult or dangerous situation), a narrative explaining the event, and a representation of the deity or saint to whom the miracle is attributed. The ex-voto, like the memorial card, has a narrative, both written and pictorial, and in this way could be seen as a historical antecedent to the modern-day memorial tattoo.

43. I interviewed various tattoo artists in Oahu for several reasons: (1) I wanted to research the tattoo memorial trend from the professional standpoint by talking with those actually inscribing the tattoo memorials on bodies, and not just those receiving them; (2) Hawaii has a good cultural amalgam of tattooing styles; its tattoo artists were trained in the Pacific (Hawaiian, Tahitian, Fijian, and Samoan styles), Asia (Japanese tattoo styles), and the United States; and (3) in addition to reflecting a variety of tattoo

training and apprenticeship, Hawaii is seen as the cutting edge of tattooing in terms of technique, style, acquisition, and regulation, and it is in many ways the American leader in the tattoo industry. Hawaii is ahead of any other state in regulating the tattoo industry, pushing for rules regarding minimum age, safety, and hygiene that other states are only just now beginning to emulate.

44. See Appendix A for my list of interview questions.

45. Ash, interview by Candi Cann, audio recording, Odyssey Tattoo, Kailua, Hawaii, June 14, 2012.

46. Dodge, interview by Candi Cann, audio recording, Koi Tattoo, Kailua, Hawaii, June 14, 2012.

47. Shane, interview by Candi Cann, audio recording, Eastside Tattoo, Kailua, Hawaii, June 14, 2012. For more on the cathartic and chemical aspects of tattooing, see D. Angus Vail, "Tattoos Are Like Potato Chips . . . You Can't Have Just One: The Process of Becoming and Being a Collector," *Deviant Behavior* 20, no. 3 (1999): 253–273, and R. M. Winchel and M. Stanley, "Self-Injurious Behavior: A Review of the Behavior and Biology of Self-Mutilation," *American Journal of Psychiatry* 148, no. 3 (1991): 306–317.

48. Lisa, interview by Candi Cann, audio recording, Koi Tattoo, Kailua, Hawaii, June 13, 2012.

49. Ibid.

50. Ash interview.

51. Two sites on DIY tattoos with cremains: "How to Use Cremation Ashes in a Memorial Tattoo," www.ehow.com/how_2156644_use-cremation-ashes-memorial-tattoo.html, and Breann Kanobi, "How to Make Tattoo Inks Out of Ashes," www.ehow.com/how_7852858_make-tattoo-inks-out-ashes.html?utm_source=dgmodule&utm_medium=2&campaign=momme1 (both accessed November 23, 2013).

52. The other shops had received requests for this but had been concerned about breaking the law by using cremains in the ink, and they thus had denied the requests. This may in part be why the instructions are given on a DIY website. The tattoo artists themselves had no problem with the request beyond meeting state regulations; they were in general fairly open-minded toward the use of ashes in tattoos.

53. Instructions for "Jailhouse Ink" are publicly available on YouTube and have over 109,000 hits. Ink can be made by burning any type of colored plastic (chess pieces, plastic razors, and so on), and then taking the residue and mixing it to become colored tattoo ink. See "Homemade Tattoo Ink Carbon Black," www.youtube.com/watch?v=tgHXKivch8I (accessed April 19, 2013).

54. Similarly, George Dickinson points out that cremains are also sometimes put into paint for pictures to be painted and framed and kept as a reminder of a loved one. For more on this, see George E. Dickinson, "Diversity in Death: Body Disposition and Memorialization," *Illness, Crisis, & Loss* 20, no. 2 (2012): 141–158.

55. Ariès, *Western Attitudes,* 66.

56. Victor Turner, *The Ritual Process: Structure and Anti-Structure* (Chicago: Aldine, 1969), 132.

57. Ariès writes that this shift is also reflected in two other trends in the changing landscape of death, dying, and mourning: first, the current practice of shielding children from death and no longer exposing them to death through visitations, funerals, and so on; and second, statistics revealing that widows commonly die within a short time of their spouses' deaths rather than remarrying. His explanation for this alarming development in widows' deaths is the fact that they are essentially left alone in their grief and not allowed the public space to grieve, whereas before, because widows were socially constricted by mourning rituals, they were able to process the death of their spouses and move on to remarry. See Ariès, *Western Attitudes,* 66.

58. Dodge interview.

59. Sigmund Freud, *On Metapsychology: The Theory of Psychoanalysis: Beyond the Pleasure Principle; The Ego and the Id and Other Works,* trans. James Strachey (New York: Penguin, 1991), 251–268.

60. Dodge interview.

61. Michel de Certeau, *The Practice of Everyday Life,* trans. Steven Rendall (Berkeley: University of California Press, 1984), 141.

3. Moving the Dead

1. Decal Junky, interview by Candi Cann, Internet chat, September 11, 2012; Brian, interview by Candi Cann, Vinyl Disorder, October 2, 2012; and Brie Keeper, e-mail interview by Candi Cann, A-1 Banner & Sign Company, April 3, 2013.

2. Charles E. Case, "Bumper Stickers and Car Signs: Ideology and Identity," *Journal of Popular Culture* 26, no. 3 (1992): 107.

3. Russell W. Belk, "Possessions and the Extended Self," *Journal of Consumer Research* 15, no. 2 (1988): 139–168.

4. Barbara B. Stern and Michael R. Solomon, "'Have You Kissed Your Professor Today?': Bumper Stickers and Consumer Self-Statements," *Advances in Consumer Research* 19, no. 1 (1992): 169–173, http://www.acrwebsite.org/search/view-conference-proceedings.aspx?Id=7289 (accessed January 1, 2014).

5. Ibid.

6. A fascinating study in 2008 illustrates the relationship between Belk's notion of extended self and the personalization of cars, noting that the more attached one is to one's vehicle (as evidenced through personalization), the more likely one is to display aggressive driving on the road. "Territoriality (as evidenced in bumper stickers, rearview mirror hanging items, car decals, custom paint jobs, etc.) was found to be significantly correlated with both at-

tachment and aggression. Participants who reported territory markers scored significantly higher on a measure of driver aggression, and participants with higher numbers of territory markers also scored significantly higher on a measure of driver aggression." William J. Szlemko et al., "Territorial Markings as a Predictor of Driver Aggression and Road Rage," *Journal of Applied Social Psychology* 38, no. 6 (2008): 1674.

7. MADD was heavily involved in lobbying the U.S. Congress to reduce the blood alcohol limit from .10 to .08. By 2000 Congress had approved this change, and by 2005 all states had enforced this new blood alcohol limit. For more on this and other legislation, visit www.madd.org.

8. Brett Buckner, "Mobile Shrines: Memorial Car Decals Are a 21st-Century Way of Expressing Grief," *Anniston (Ala.) Star,* July 3, 2011, http://annistonstar.com/view/full_story/14544787/article-Mobile-shrines —Memorial-car-decals-are-a-21st-century-way-of-expressing-grief? instance=home_lifestyle#ixzz2LdwmrOCs (accessed February 12, 2013).

9. Bloch, "Mobile Discourse." The reader will note, also, that this predates the practice of car-decal memorialization by at least six years, though it follows the high prevalence of bumper stickers used in the late 1980s by MADD.

10. In one rather interesting blog that I came across, there was a discussion of how to "treat" someone who had a car-decal memorial on her or his vehicle. One person suggested paying that person's toll on tollways or parking fees in parking lots, whereas others felt it rather confusing and a violation of others' rights to privacy to display car-decal memorials in public. Regardless of one's opinion, however, there is no denial that this is a cultural trend that seems to be increasing rather than disappearing.

11. Christenfeld is quoted in Steve Schmidt, "Car Culture Sees Decals as Mobile Memorials," *UT San Diego,* May 3, 2010, www.utsandiego .com/news/2010/may/03/car-culture-sees-decals-as-mobile-memorials /?print&page=all (accessed February 22, 2013).

12. Allison Engel, "In the Rear Window, Tributes to the Dead," *New York Times,* December 11, 2005, www.nytimes.com/2005/12/11/fashion/ sundaystyles/11DECALS.html?_r=0 (accessed February 12, 2013).

13. Decal Junky, interview by Candi Cann, Internet chat, September 11, 2012.

14. Ibid.

15. Brian, Vinyl Disorder, interview.

16. Buckner, "Mobile Shrines."

17. In a conversation on September 7, 2013, at the conference titled "Death, Dying, and Disposal" at the Open University in England, Pamela Roberts pointed out that in her research she did not find that the decals were removed; in fact, their removal was not discussed. See Pamela Roberts and Lourdes A. Vidal, "Perpetual Care in Cyberspace: A Portrait of Memorials on the Web," *Omega: A Journal of Death and Dying* 40, no. 4 (2000): 521–546.

18. I am indebted to John Alford for this point.

19. Tanya Bricking, "Memorial Car Decals: In Honor of Lost Loved Ones," *Honolulu Advertiser,* July 24, 2002, http://the.honoluluadvertiser.com/article/2002/Jul/24/il/il01a.html (accessed February 22, 2013).

20. This being said, I did not conduct fieldwork in Mexico on this phenomenon, and because of the proximity between Mexico and California (where many believe this phenomenon to have originated), I would argue that there might be evidence of car-decal memorialization in Mexico.

21. The popularity of the T-shirt in American fashion is generally traced to the U.S. Navy uniform, which then also became de rigueur for the U.S. Army. When American sailors and soldiers returned to the United States at the end of World War II, the T-shirt came with them, entering everyday American life and becoming a popular clothing staple. Charles Osgood, "A Short History of the T-Shirt," *CBS News,* July 9, 2006, www.cbsnews.com/video/watch/?id=1786690n (accessed February 18, 2013).

22. There are numerous Steve Jobs memorial T-shirts for sale on eBay: www.ebay.com/itm/Steve-Jobs-Apple_LOGO-T-Shirt-tee-RIP-tribute-memorial-/14061688293 (accessed November 25, 2013).

23. A variety of Whitney Houston memorial T-shirts is available on eBay: www.ebay.com/sch/i.html?_trksid=p5197.m570.11313&_nkw=whitney+houston+memorial+t-shirt&_sacat=0 (accessed November 25, 2013).

24. "Design Memorial T-Shirts Online," www.customink.com/t-shirts/memorial-t-shirts.html (accessed November 25, 2013), and "Memorial," http://shop.cafepress.com/memorial (accessed November 25, 2013), are two popular websites that offer do-it-yourself memorial T-shirts that can be ordered individually or in bulk.

25. Kyle K., interview by Candi Cann, audio recording, CustomInk, live chat, September 6, 2012.

26. Ibid.

27. Jenn Shreve, "A Fitting Memorial: The Growing Popularity of the Memorial T-Shirt," *Slate.com,* August 26, 2003, www.slate.com/articles/news_and_politics/the_gist/2003/08/a_fitting_memorial.html (accessed January 12, 2013).

28. Ibid.

29. J. E. Newhagen and M. Ancell, "The Expression of Emotion and Social Status in the Language of Bumper Stickers," *Journal of Language and Social Psychology* 14, no. 3 (1995): 313.

30. Robert Andrew Powell, "Fitting Tribute," *Mother Jones,* May–June 2007, 58–63.

31. Dan Morse, "Fraught Couture: Shirts for the Dead Are the New Rag in Some Inner Cities. They Memorialize Victims of Violence; Do They Glorify the Thug Life? 'More T-Shirts Than Friends,'" *Wall Street Journal,* February 4, 1999, A1.

32. Ibid.

33. Kate Moser, "New Memorials: T-Shirts, Websites, Auto Decals," *Christian Science Monitor,* May 25, 2006, 15.

4. Speaking to the Dead

1. See www.facebook.com/AuroraTheaterShooting (accessed November 26, 2013).

2. "Newtown Memorial Fund," http://newtownmemorialfund. org, and the following Facebook sites are active memorial websites: "R.I.P. Sandy Hook Elementary School Children," www.facebook.com/ RIPSandyHookElementaryChildren; "RIP Sandy Hook Elementary Victims," www.facebook.com/SandyRIPHook?fref=ts; "Memorial Page for the Victims at Sandy Hook Elementary," www.facebook .com/121412NEWTOWNCT; "Sandy Hook Promise," www.facebook .com/SandyHookPromise?fref=ts; "Sandy Hook Elementary School," www .facebook.com/SandyHook12.14.12?fref=ts; "Sandy Hook Elementary School Massacre Memorial Page," www.facebook.com/pages/Sandy-Hook-Elementary-School-Massacre-Memorial-Page/142591449223701?fref=ts; "In Loving Memory of Sandy Hook Elementary Victims," www .facebook.com/ILMSHEV?fref=ts (all accessed November 26, 2013). The domain names SandyHookMemorial.com, NewtownMemorial.org, and sandyhookmemorial.org are reserved, to be activated once the funds and dissemination of the funds have been determined.

3. See the Youtube video of the animated tattoo linked to a QR code at www.youtube.com/watch?v=f3qv2dSXQXk (accessed November 26, 2013).

4. Dignity's memorials are tied to the funeral package and include the ability to light a virtual candle, to give gifts such as teddy bears (in various colors), and to offer flowers in memory of the deceased, as well as to write a message directly to or in memory of the deceased. "Dignity Memorial," www.dignitymemorial .com/dm20/en_US/main/dm/index.page (accessed November 26, 2013).

5. This was an informal survey, conducted in the fall of 2011, of all funeral homes within a fifty-mile radius of Waco proper; it consisted mainly of asking funeral home personnel about their Internet memorialization services.

6. Quiring Headstones provides "living headstones" with microchip technology that allows people to communicate "regardless of where they live." Quiring Monuments, www.monuments.com/living-headstones (accessed November 26, 2013).

7. See my "Tombstone Technology: Deathscapes in Asia, the U.K. and the U.S," in *Digital Legacy and Interaction: Post-Mortem Issues*, ed. Cristiano Maciel and Vinícius Carvalho Pereira (New York: Springer, 2013), 101–113.

8. Sea burials are also found in the United States; one company, Eternal

Reef, offers concrete reef interment of cremains. See Rachel Saslow, "Green Burials Return Dead to the Earth," *Washington Post,* June 12, 2011.

9. Lily Kong, "No Place, New Places: Death and Its Rituals in Urban Asia," *Urban Studies* 49, no. 2 (2012): 430.

10. Wang is quoted in Liu Lu, "Virtual Memorial," *China Daily,* April 1, 2011, http://usa.chinadaily.com.cn/life/2011-04/01/content_12262543.htm (accessed March 15, 2012).

11. Plots in Hong Kong, for example, are purchased for a term, after which families must either cremate the bodies to make room for more burials or consent to moving family members to smaller graves (once the bodies have decomposed) in order to accommodate the large number of dead needing access to the burial grounds.

12. "Internet World Statistics, China," http://www.internetworldstats. com/asia/cn.htm (accessed November 26, 2013).

13. "Lifenaut Blog," http://lifenaut.com/blog/ (accessed November 26, 2013).

14. See my "Tombstone Technology."

15. Approximately 17 percent of Americans visit a loved one's grave site following the funeral and burial. See Gary Laderman, *Rest in Peace: A Cultural History of Death and the Funeral Home in Twentieth-Century America* (New York: Oxford University Press, 2003).

16. See Brian Carroll and Katie Landry, "Logging On and Letting Out: Using Online Social Networks to Grieve and to Mourn," *Bulletin of Science, Technology and Society* 30, no. 5 (2010): 341–349.

17. Jenna Wortham, "As Facebook Users Die, Ghosts Reach Out," *New York Times,* July 17, 2010, http://www.nytimes.com/2010/07/18/ technology/18death.html (accessed February 27, 2012).

18. Caleb Johnson, "How to 'Memorialize' the Facebook Pages of the Recently Deceased," *Huffington Post,* October 27, 2009, www.switched. com/2009/10/27/memorialize-the-facebook-pages-of-friends-who-pass-away/ (accessed February 22, 2012).

19. These industries, which are beyond the scope of this chapter, are growing exponentially, and a brief but incomplete list can be found at the digital beyond.com, www.thedigitalbeyond.com/online-services-list/ (accessed February 24, 2012). Various organizations concerned with access to digital information following one's demise include AfterSteps, AssetLock, Dead Man's Switch, Death Switch, E-Z-Safe, Entrust, EstateLogic, Eternity Message, GreatGoodbye, Legacy Organiser, LifeEnsured, Lifestrand, Memento Mori, My Last Email, My Web Will, PartingWishes, PasswordBox, SecureSafe, and VitalLock.

20. See www.mydeathspace.com.

21. See Robert Dobler, "Ghosts in the Machine: Mourning the MySpace Dead," in *Folklore and the Internet: Vernacular Expression in a Digital*

World, ed. Trevor J. Blank (Logan: Utah State University Press, 2009), 175–193.

22. Xu Lin, "Virtually Immortal," *China Daily,* December 14, 2011, www.chinadaily.com.cn/cndy/2011-12/14/content_14261197.htm (accessed February 28, 2012).

23. Wang Hongyi, "Funeral Packed for Young Couple," *China Daily,* August 5, 2011, www.chinadaily.com.cn/china/201108/05/content_13053836.htm&title=Funeral%20packed%20for%20young%20couple%7CSociety%7Cchinadaily.com.cn (accessed February 28, 2012). One example is this comment from Thomas (not his real name) on the China Daily Forum: "May they rest in perfect peace. This should be a great lesson for the corrupt in the society. I know readers are fed up with investigations upon investigations but I'm sure that something better will come out from this. This fatal accipdent [*sic*] has exposed China's fast developmental projects and the corrupt in the society. . . . Long Live China"; http://comment.chinadaily.com.cn/articlecmt.shtml?url=http://www.chinadaily.com.cn/china/201108/05/content_13053836.htm&title=Funeral%20packed%20for%20young%20couple%7CSociety%7Cchinadaily.com.cn (accessed February 28, 2012).

24. See www.desaparecidos.org and http://carlosmugica.com.ar/, respectively. For more on Mugica, see Cann, "Holy Wars, Cold Wars and Dirty Wars.

25. "When compared to markets globally, Argentina's users average the second highest amount of time on Facebook.com behind Israel—where visitors averaged 10.6 hours during April." See "Facebook Users in Argentina Spend 9 Hours a Month on Site, Second Only to Israel in User Engagement," *comScore,* June 9, 2011, www.comscore.com/Press_Events/Press_Releases/2011/6/Facebook_Users_in_Argentina_Spend_9_Hours_a_Month_on_Site (accessed March 16, 2012).

26. I have written more extensively on this in "Virtual Memorials: Bereavement and the Internet," in *Our Changing Journey to the End: Reshaping Death, Dying, and Grief in America,* ed. Christina Staudt and J. Harold Ellens, 2 vols. (Santa Barbara, Calif.: Praeger, 2013), 1:193–206.

27. More research needs to be done linking material remembrance with virtual remembrance, and there are some examples in Latin America, though these tend to be more political in nature. One such example is the Blue Heart movement in Panama, whereby blue hearts are painted at the sites of traffic accidents to raise awareness and to decrease traffic fatalities. Online sites describe the incidents and nature of the fatalities, though the hearts themselves do not contain web pages or Internet links. See Zenaida Vásquez, "En recuerdo a víctimas de accidente," August 21, 2009, www.panamaamerica.com.pa/notas/820983-en-recuerdo-a-victimas-de-accidente (accessed January 5, 2014).

28. Geoffrey Galt Harpham, *The Ascetic Imperative in Culture and Criticism* (Chicago: University of Chicago Press, 1987), 14.

29. Conversation between anonymous widow and Candi Cann at Columbia University seminar on death, March 2012.

30. Jacques Derrida, *The Work of Mourning,* ed. Pascale-Anne Brault and Michael Naas (Chicago: University of Chicago Press, 2001), 55.

31. E-mail correspondence with Donald Joralemon, March 2012.

32. I am indebted here to Donald Joralemon for helping me see this distinction in language.

33. "Yolanda S. Cuevas, In Memoriam," *Waco Tribune-Herald,* April 25, 2013, www.legacy.com/ns/obitfinder/obituary-search.aspx?daterange=2010-2013&firstname=yolanda&lastname=cuevas&countryid=1&stateid=57&affiliateid=all (accessed November 27, 2013).

34. "Recordatorios: Laura Raimon," *La Nacion,* April 25, 2013, http://servicios.lanacion.com.ar/edicion-impresa/avisos-funebres/resultado/categorias=1037,1039-fecha=20130425-pagina=1-palabra= (accessed April 26, 2013). The original Spanish is as follows: "Raiman, Laura.—A 10 años de tu partida, te extrañamos profundamente y expresamos nuestro eterno amor a tu memoria. Tus padres Hilda y Federico, tus hermanos, Nora y Horacio, tus cuñados Karina y Ricardo y tus sobrinas Candela, Victoria y Lucía que, aunque no pudieron conocerte, te tienen presente en sus vidas." (Author's translation.)

35. These are all different, though popular ways of writing emoticons, some of which are recognized as shortcuts to a sad face graphic, and others simply are a representation of a sad face.

36. The number of people "talking about" a Facebook page reveals the traffic an Internet site receives, while "likes" make a page a permanent part of one's Facebook archive. The fact that so many people are discussing the page is indicative of the page's high profile following the Boston Marathon bombings.

37. Victor Turner, *From Ritual to Theatre: The Human Seriousness of Play* (New York: Performing Arts Journal Publications, 1982), 99.

38. Doss, *Memorial Mania,* 2.

39. According to Daniel Boorstin, a consumption community "consists of people who have a feeling of shared well-being, shared risks, common interests and common concerns that come from consuming the same kinds of objects." Daniel J. Boorstin, "Welcome to the Consumption Community," in Boorstin, *The Decline of Radicalism: Reflections on America Today* (New York: Random House, 1969), 22; Michael Davis, "Boorstin Proposes New Concept of 'Communities of Consumption,'" *Rice Thresher* (Rice University student newspaper), December 9, 1965, 3.

40. Fauna, "Wenzhou Train Crash: Police Captain's Insistence Saves Girl," *ChinaSmack,* July 27, 2011, www.chinasmack.com/2011/stories/wenzhou-

train-crash-police-captain-shao-yerong-saves-yiyi.html (accessed February, 28 2012). Readers interested in the original Chinese text should see the website.

41. "R.I.P. Juan Carlos (calaberilla) Raya," www.facebook.com/pages/ RIP-Juan-Carlos-calaberilla-Raya/216657528383451 (accessed January 1, 2013). Original text in Spanish is as follows: "Eras unicoo J . . . Tu no te meresias estoo. . . . Pero el ke te hiso esto va pagar muyy caro!! Te keremos muchisisisimoooo.! Siempre vas a estar en nuestros corazoness No tengo mucho ke te conoci pero fue lo suficiente para saber ke eras una buena persona. . . . Come te voy a extranarr ;(((. . Descanza en paz . . We love you —J——." (Author's translation.)

42. Ibid. Original text in Spanish as follows: "E—— No puedo creer esto que te pasó te. No tedigo adios por que siempre bas estar en el corazón de todas las personas que te conocimos." (Author's translation.)

43. See Sherry Turkle's work on sex and the Internet in *Life on the Screen: Identity in the Age of the Internet* (New York: Simon & Schuster, 1995) for a deeper discussion of virtual reality and "other" realities.

44. Cathy Lynn Grossman, "'Today We Are All Hokies' on Facebook," *USA Today,* April 17, 2007, discusses the trend of memorializing through posting one's picture with the deceased as one's Facebook photo. This practice identifies grievers as a community, much as the Victorian mourning practice of wearing a black armband did.

5. Grieving the Dead in Alternative Spaces

1. Neither Judaism nor Islam permits embalmment or cremation (though some Jews now practice embalmment for the sake of convenience), and though the body is quickly buried in Islam (usually within twenty-four hours), the family is generally part of the burial process, washing, preparing, and dressing the body for burial. There is also a rich martyrological tradition in Islam that, like Roman Catholicism, allows for a continued relationship with the dead. Judaism prescribes the practice of sitting shiva for the dead, an extended mourning period. Though Judaism doesn't have a vivid notion of an afterlife, it has a rich memorialization tradition that includes the regular commemoration of the dead by the lighting of a Yahrzeit candle on holidays, anniversaries of deaths, and so on.

2. See George E. Dickinson and Heath C. Hoffmann, "Roadside Memorial Policies in the United States," *Mortality* 15, no. 2 (2010): 154–167; Catherine Ann Collins and Alexandra Opie, "When Places Have Agency: Roadside Shrines as Traumascapes," *Continuum: Journal of Media & Cultural Studies* 24, no. 1 (2010): 107–118.

3. Alan Dundes, "Thinking Ahead: A Folkloristic Reflection of the Future Orientation in American Worldview," *Anthropological Quarterly* 42, no. 2 (1969): 65.

4. Conversation with Anna Beal, May 10, 2013.

5. Victor Turner defines *communitas* in this passage: "What is interesting about liminal phenomena for our present purposes is the blend they offer of lowliness and sacredness, of homogeneity and comradeship. We are presented, in such rites, with a 'moment in and out of time,' and in and out of secular social structure, which reveals, however fleetingly, some recognition (in symbol if not always in language) of a generalized social bond that has ceased to be and has simultaneously yet to be fragmented into a multiplicity of structural ties. These are the ties organized in terms either of caste, class, or rank hierarchies or of segmentary oppositions in the stateless societies beloved of political anthropologists. It is as though there are here two major 'models' for human interrelatedness, juxtaposed and alternating. The first is of society as a structured, differentiated, and often hierarchical system of politico-legaleconomic positions with many types of evaluation, separating men in terms of 'more or less.' The second, which emerges recognizably in the liminal period, is of society as an unstructured or rudimentarily structured and relatively undifferentiated *communitas,* community, or even communion of equal individuals who submit together to the general authority of the ritual elders." Turner, *The Ritual Process,* 96.

6. Bobby C. Alexander, "Correcting Misinterpretations of Turner's Theory: An African-American Pentecostal Illustration," *Journal for the Scientific Study of Religion* 30, no. 1 (March 1991): 27.

7. The one exception to this seems to be an exclusion of killers, however, evidenced by the treatment of Eric Harris and Dylan Klebold (the boys responsible for the Columbine killings), Adam Lanza (the Sandy Hook killer), and Tamerlan Tsarnaev, one of the Boston Marathon bombers. Only the Amish seem to have included the family of Charles Carl Roberts, the killer responsible for the Nickel Mines tragedy, in their bereavement process.

8. The only possible exception here might be tattoos that are inked in nonvisible areas, though the actual tattoo itself is often not visible to the person wearing the tattoo (for example, when it is on the back), so in some ways it remains a visible sign, whether its visibility is limited to a particular (intimate) audience or a wider one.

9. Elizabeth Hallam and Jenny Hockey, *Death, Memory, and Material Culture* (New York: Berg, 2001), 99.

10. Jean Baudrillard, "The Finest Consumer Object: The Body," in *The Body: A Reader,* ed. Miriam Fraser and Monica Greco (New York: Routledge, 2005), 282; emphasis in original.

Bibliography

Ablon, Joan. "Bereavement in a Samoan Community." *British Journal of Medical Psychology* 44, no. 4 (1971): 329–337.

———. "The Samoan Funeral in Urban America." *Ethnology* 9, no. 3 (1970): 209–227.

"Abu Dawud Book 028, Hadith Number 4157." *Haddith Collection.* www. hadithcollection.com/abudawud/260-Abu%20Dawud%20Book%20 28.%20Combing%20The%20Hair/17960-abu-dawud-book-028-hadith-number-4157.html (accessed May 5, 2013).

Alex⸺ ⸺obby C. "Correcting Misinterpretations of Turner's Theory: ⸺n-American Pentecostal Illustration." *Journal for the Scientific ⸺eligion* 30, no. 1 (March 1991): 26–44.

⸺ Facebook Page." www.facebook.com/pages/RIP-Andy- ⸺043709994 (accessed November 29, 2013).

⸺*he Hour of Our Death.* Translated by Helen Weaver. New ⸺989.

⸺*titudes toward Death: From the Middle Ages to the Pres-* ⸺⸺ by Patricia M. Ranum. Baltimore: Johns Hopkins Univer- ⸺ ress, 1974.

Ash. Interview by Candi Cann. Audio recording. Odyssey Tattoo, Kailua, Hawaii, June 14, 2012.

Asmar, Melanie. "Aurora Century Theater Reopens Six Months after Shootings with Speeches, *The Hobbit.*" *Denver Westword,* January 18, 2013. http://blogs.westword.com/latestword/2013/01/aurora_century_theater_ reopens_the_hobbit_photos.php (accessed March 18, 2013).

Aurora History Museum. www.auroragov.org/ThingsToDo/ArtsandCulture/ AuroraHistoryMuseum/index.htm (accessed November 20, 2013).

"Aurora Shooting Memorial: Community in Early Talks of What to Do with Century 16 Theater, Reflects on Columbine." *Huffington Post,* July 31, 2012. www.huffingtonpost.com/2012/07/31/aurora-shooting-memorial- _n_1723565.html (accessed April 2, 2013).

Averill, J. R., and E. P. Nunley. "Grief as an Emotion and as a Disease: A Social-Constructionist Perspective." In *Handbook of Bereavement: Theory, Research, and Intervention,* edited by Margaret S. Stroebe, Wolfgang Stroebe, and Robert O. Hansson. New York: Cambridge University Press, 1993.

Baptist, Karen Wilson. "Diaspora: Death without a Landscape." *Mortality* 15, no. 4 (2010): 294–307.

Barnes, John. *Evita, First Lady: A Biography of Eva Peron.* New York: Grove Press, 1978.

Baudrillard, Jean. "The Finest Consumer Object: The Body." In *The Body: A Reader,* edited by Miriam Fraser and Monica Greco. New York: Routledge, 2005, 277–282.

———. *Simulacra and Simulation.* Translated by Sheila Faria Glaser. Ann Arbor: University of Michigan Press, 1994.

Belk, Russell W. "Possessions and the Extended Self." *Journal of Consumer Research* 15, no. 2 (1988): 139–168.

Berkowitz, Philip M., Thomas Müller-Bonanni, and Anders Etgen Reitz. *International Labor and Employment Law: Labor and Employment Law in Argentina.* Chicago: American Bar Association, 2006.

Billones, Cherrie Lou. "18th Anniversary of Aum Shinrikyo Subway Gas Attack Remembered in Tokyo." *Japan Daily Press,* March 20, 2013. http://japandailypress.com/18th-anniversary-of-aum-shinrikyo-subway-gas-attack-remembered-in-tokyo-2025515 (accessed May 8, 2013).

Bloch, Linda-Renée. "Mobile Discourse: Political Bumper Stickers as a Communication Event in Israel." *Journal of Communication* 50, no. 2 (2000): 48–76.

Bolick, Kate. "A Death on Facebook." *Atlantic Monthly,* September 2010, 35–36.

Boorstin, Daniel J. "Welcome to the Consumption Community." In Boorstin, *The Decline of Radicalism: Reflections on America Today.* New York: Random House, 1969.

Bradley, James. "Body Commodification? Class and Tattoos in Victorian Britain." In *Written on the Body: The Tattoo in European and American History,* edited by Jane Caplan. Princeton: Princeton University Press, 2000, 136–155.

Brandes, Stanley. "Sugar, Colonialism, and Death: On the Origins of Mexico's Day of the Dead." *Comparative Studies in Society and History* 39, no. 2 (1997): 270–299.

Brian. E-mail interview by Candi Cann. Vinyl Disorder, October 2, 2012.

Bricking, Tanya. "Memorial Car Decals: In Honor of Lost Loved Ones." *Honolulu Advertiser,* July 24, 2002. http://the.honoluluadvertiser.com/article/2002/Jul/24/il/il01a.html (accessed February 22, 2013).

Brier, Norman. "Grief Following Miscarriage: A Comprehensive Review of the Literature." *Journal of Women's Health* 17, no. 3 (April 2008): 451–464.

Brody, B., and A. Halevy. "Brain Death: Reconciling Definitions, Criteria, and Tests." *Annals of Internal Medicine* 119, no. 6 (1993): 519–525.

Bronner, Simon J. "Digitizing and Virtualizing Folklore." In *Folklore and the Internet: Vernacular Expression in a Digital World,* edited by Trevor Blank. Logan: Utah State University Press, 2009, 21–66.

Buckner, Brett. "Mobile Shrines: Memorial Car Decals Are a 21st-Century Way of Expressing Grief." *Anniston (Ala.) Star,* July 3, 2011. http://annistonstar.com/view/full_story/14544787/article-Mobile-shrines—Memorial-car-decals-are-a-21st-century-way-of-expressing-grief?instance=home_lifestyle#ixzz2LdwmrOCs (accessed February 12, 2013).

Byrne, Mark. "Around the Corner of Loss." *New York Times,* April 1, 2012.

Cann, Candi K. "Holy Wars, Cold Wars and Dirty Wars: Manufacturing Martyrs in the Two-thirds World: A Case Study." Ph.D. diss., Harvard University, 2009.

———. "Tombstone Technology: Deathscapes in Asia, the U.K. and the U.S." In *Digital Legacy and Interaction: Post-Mortem Issues,* edited by Cristiano Maciel and Vinícius Carvalho Pereira. New York: Springer, 2013, 101–113.

———. "Virtual Memorials: Bereavement and the Internet." In *Our Changing Journey to the End: Reshaping Death, Dying, and Grief in America,* edited by Christina Staudt and J. Harold Ellens. 2 vols. Santa Barbara, Calif.: Praeger, 2013, 1:193–206

Caplan, Jane, ed. *Written on the Body: The Tattoo in European and American History.* Princeton: Princeton University Press, 2000.

Carlson, Prescott. "The Man behind the Crosses." *Miscellaneous,* February 17, 2008. http://chicagoist.com/2008/02/17/whos_leaving_th.php (accessed March 16, 2013).

Carroll, Brian, and Katie Landry. "Logging On and Letting Out: Using Online Social Networks to Grieve and to Mourn." *Bulletin of Science, Technology and Society* 30, no. 5 (2010): 341–349.

Case, Charles E. "Bumper Stickers and Car Signs Ideology and Identity." *Journal of Popular Culture* 26 (1992): 107–119.

Castellanos, Sara. "City Removes Items from Temporary Aurora Theater Shooting Memorial." *Aurora Sentinel,* September 20, 2012. www.aurorasentinel.com/news/metroaurora/removal/ (accessed April 7, 2013).

Caswell, Glenys. "Personalisation in Scottish Funerals: Individualised Ritual or Relational Process?" *Mortality* 16, no. 3 (2011): 242–258.

Chapple, Alison, and Sue Ziebland. "How the Internet Is Changing the Experience of Bereavement by Suicide: A Qualitative Study in the UK." *Health: An Interdisciplinary Journal for the Social Study of Health, Illness and Medicine* 15, no. 2 (2011): 173–187.

Chartier, Roger. *On the Edge of the Cliff: History, Language, and Practices.* Baltimore: Johns Hopkins University Press, 1997.

Cheung, Christy M. K., Pui-Yee Chiu, and Matthew K. O. Lee. "Online Social Networks: Why Do Students Use Facebook?" *Computers in Human Behavior* 27, no. 4 (2011): 1337–1343.

Clark, Jennifer, and Majella Franzmann. "Authority from Grief, Presence and Place in the Making of Roadside Memorials." *Death Studies* 30, no. 6 (2006): 579–599.

Collins, Catherine Ann, and Alexandra Opie. "When Places Have Agency: Roadside Shrines as Traumascapes." *Continuum: Journal of Media & Cultural Studies* 24, no. 1 (2010): 107–118.

"Conn. Governor: 'Evil Visited This Community.'" Associated Press, December 14, 2012. http://on.aol.com/video/conn—governor—evil-visited-this-community-517599663 (accessed March 21, 2013).

Conrad, Fred R. "Journey's End." *New York Times,* November 26, 2006.

Coogan, Michael D., Marc Z. Brettler, Carol Ann Newsom, and Pheme Perkins, eds. *The New Oxford Annotated Bible with the Apocrypha: New Revised Standard Version.* New York: Oxford University Press, 2010.

Crowder, Linda Sun. "Chinese Funerals in San Francisco Chinatown: American Chinese Expressions in Mortuary Ritual Performance." *Journal of American Folklore* 113, no. 450 (2000): 451–463.

DasGupta, Sayantani, and Marsha Hurst. "Death in Cyberspace: Bodies, Boundaries, and Postmodern Memorializing." In *The Many Ways We Talk about Death in Contemporary Society: Interdisciplinary Studies in Portrayal and Classification,* edited by Margaret Souza and Christina Staudt. Lewiston, N.Y.: Edwin Mellen, 2009, 105–120.

Davies, Douglas J. *Death, Ritual and Belief: The Rhetoric of Funerary Rites.* 2nd ed. New York: Continuum, 2002.

Davis, Michael. "Boorstin Proposes New Concept of 'Communities of Consumption.'" *Rice Thresher* (Rice University student newspaper), December 9, 1965, 3.

Decal Junky. Interview by Candi Cann. Internet chat. September 11, 2012.

de Certeau, Michel. *The Practice of Everyday Life.* Berkeley: University of California Press, 1984.

DeMello, Margo. "Part 46." In DeMello, *Encyclopedia of Body Adornment.* Westport, Conn.: Greenwood, 2007.

Derrida, Jacques. *The Work of Mourning.* Edited by Pascale-Anne Brault and Michael Naas. Chicago: University of Chicago Press, 2001.

Dickinson, George E. "Diversity in Death: Body Disposition and Memorialization." *Illness, Crisis & Loss* 20, no. 2 (2012): 141–158.

Dickinson, George E., and Heath C. Hoffmann. "Roadside Memorial Policies in the United States." *Mortality* 15, no. 2 (2010): 154–167.

"Dignity Memorial." www.dignitymemorial.com/dm20/en_US/main/dm/index.page (accessed November 26, 2013).

Dinter, Maarten Hesselt van. *The World of Tattoo: An Illustrated History.* Amsterdam: KIT, 2005.

Dobler, Robert Thomas. "Ghost Bikes." In *Grassroots Memorials: The Pol-*

itics of Memorializing Traumatic Death, edited by Peter Jan Margry and Cristina Sánchez-Carretero. New York: Berghahn Books, 2011, 169–187.

———. "Ghosts in the Machine: Mourning the MySpace Dead." In *Folklore and the Internet: Vernacular Expression in a Digital World,* edited by Trevor J. Blank. Logan: Utah State University Press, 2009, 175–193.

Dodge. Interview by Candi Cann. Audio recording. Koi Tattoo, Kailua, Hawaii, June 14, 2012.

Doka, Kenneth J., ed. *Disenfranchised Grief.* Lexington, Mass.: Lexington Books/D. C. Heath, 1989.

Doss, Erika. *Memorial Mania: Public Feeling in America.* Chicago: University of Chicago Press, 2010.

DSM 5. www.dsm5.org/ Pages/default.aspx.

"Do You Mind Showing Me Your Memorial Tattoo?" Community Forum, The Bump. http://forums.thebump.com/discussion/7764074/do-you-mind-showing-me-your-memorial-tattoo.

Dubee, Bryce S. "Japanese Water Parks Banning People with Tattoos from Entering Premises." *Stars and Stripes,* July 12, 2008. www.stripes .com/news/japanese-water-parks-banning-people-with-tattoos-from-entering-premises-1.80904 (accessed May 7, 2013).

Dundes, Alan. "The Number Three in American Culture." In Dundes, *Every Man His Way: Readings in Cultural Anthropology.* Englewood Cliffs, N.J.: Prentice-Hall, 1968, 401–424.

———. "Thinking Ahead: A Folkloristic Reflection of the Future Orientation in American Worldview." *Anthropological Quarterly* 42, no. 2 (1969): 53–72.

Engel, Allison. "In the Rear Window, Tributes to the Dead." *New York Times,* December 11, 2005. www.nytimes.com/2005/12/11/fashion/ sundaystyles/11DECALS.html?_r=0 (accessed February 12, 2013).

Engel, George L. "Grief and Grieving." *AJN: American Journal of Nursing* 64, no. 9 (1964): 93–98.

Ettinger, Yair. "Son Gets Dad's Auschwitz Tattoo on Own Arm." *Haaretz,* January 5, 2008.

Fauna. "Wenzhou Train Crash: Police Captain's Insistence Saves Girl." *ChinaSmack,* July 27, 2011. www.chinasmack.com/2011/stories/ wenzhou-train-crash-police-captain-shao-yerong-saves-yiyi.html (accessed February 28, 2012).

Feng, W. E. I. "On the Song Military System: A Case from Tattoo." *Journal of Historical Science* 9 (2005): 008.

Finlay, Christopher J., and Guenther Krueger. "A Space for Mothers: Grief as Identity Construction on Memorial Websites Created by SIDS Parents." *Omega: Journal of Death and Dying* 63, no. 1 (2011): 21–44.

Forward, The, and Ron Dicker. "Jews with Tattoos." *Haaretz,* October 11,

2009. www.haaretz.com/jewish-world/2.209/jews-with-tattoos-1.6313 (accessed April 18, 2013).

Franzmann, Majella. "Highway to Heaven: The Cosmology of Roadside Memorials." Paper presented at the First International Symposium on Roadside Memorials, University of New England, Australia, June 25–27, 2004.

Freud, Sigmund. *On Metapsychology: The Theory of Psychoanalysis: Beyond the Pleasure Principle; The Ego and the Id and Other Works.* Translated by James Strachey. New York: Penguin Books, 1991.

Fullard-Leo, Betty. "Body Art." *Coffee Times,* Spring–Summer 1999. http:// coffeetimes.com/tattoos.htm (accessed November 29, 2013).

G., Donna (alias). Interview by Candi Cann. Audio recording. Kailua, Hawaii, March 9, 2011.

Ghostbikes. "Ghostbikes: How To." http://ghostbikes.org/howto (accessed November 20, 2013).

Graves, Karen Elizabeth. "Social Networking Sites and Grief: An Exploratory Investigation of Potential Benefits." Ph.D. diss., Indiana University of Pennsylvania, 2009.

Greenberg, Joel. "Israel's Bumper-Sticker Wars: Counterattack from the Right." *New York Times,* March 3, 1996.

Grider, Sylvia. "Memorializing Shooters with Their Victims." In *Grassroots Memorials: The Politics of Memorializing Traumatic Death,* edited by Peter Jan Margry and Cristina Sánchez-Carretero. New York: Berghahn Books, 2011, 114–120.

———. "Public Grief and the Politics of Memorial: Contesting the Memory of 'the Shooters' at Columbine High School." *Anthropology Today* 23, no. 3 (2007): 3–7.

Griffith, Christopher. "Ghost Riders." *New York Magazine,* June 23, 2008, 28–35.

Grossman, Cathy Lynn. "'Today We Are All Hokies' on Facebook." *USA Today,* April 17, 2007.

Guerin, Lisa. *Employment Law: The Essential HR Desk Reference.* Berkeley, Calif.: Nolo, 2011.

Gundaker, Grey. "At Home on the Other Side: African American Burials as Commemorative Landscapes." In *Places of Commemoration: Search for Identity and Landscape Design,* edited by J. Wolschke-Bulmahn. Washington, D.C.: Dumbarton Oaks, 2001, 25–54.

Hallam, Elizabeth, and Jenny Hockey. *Death, Memory and Material Culture.* New York: Berg, 2001.

Haney, C. A., C. Leimer, and J. Lowery. "Spontaneous Memorialization: Violent Death and Emerging Mourning Ritual." *Omega* 35 (1997): 159–171.

Harrison, R. P. *The Dominion of the Dead.* Chicago: University of Chicago Press, 2003.

Hentz, Patricia. "The Body Remembers: Grieving and a Circle of Time." *Qualitative Health Research* 12, no. 2 (2002): 161–172.

Hieftje, Kimberly. "The Role of Social Networking Sites as a Medium for Memorialization in Emerging Adults." Ph.D. diss., Indiana University, 2009.

"Homemade Tattoo Ink Carbon Black." www.youtube.com/watch?v=tgHXKivch8I (accessed April 19, 2013).

"How to Use Cremation Ashes in a Memorial Tattoo." www.ehow.com/how_2156644_use-cremation-ashes-memorial-tattoo.html (accessed November 23, 2013).

Hunter, Christopher, Louisa Lam, and Ketong Lin. Employment Law in China. 2nd ed. Hong Kong: CCH Hong Kong Limited, 2008.

Igou, Brad. "Amish Country News." www.amishnews.com/amisharticles/religioustraditions.htm#Part%20Six:%20The%20Funeral%20Service (accessed March 15, 2013).

"Infants Remembered in Silence." www.irisremembers.com/memories/memorialtattoos.cfm (accessed November 22, 2013).

"In Loving Memory of Sandy Hook Elementary Victims." www.facebook.com/ILMSHEV?fref=ts (accessed November 29, 2013).

Irwin, Katherine. "Legitimating the First Tattoo: Moral Passage through Informal Interaction." Symbolic Interaction 24, no. 1 (2001): 49–73.

Johnson, Caleb. "How to 'Memorialize' the Facebook Pages of the Recently Deceased." Huffington Post, October 27, 2009. www.switched.com/2009/10/27/memorialize-the-facebook-pages-of-friends-who-pass-away/ (accessed February 22, 2012).

Jun, L. I. U. "A First Probe into the Tattoo on the Face in Dulong Ethnic Group." Journal of the Central University for Nationalities (Philosophy and Social Sciences Edition) 6 (2007): 015.

Kanobi, Breann. "How to Make Tattoo Inks Out of Ashes." www.ehow.com/how_7852858_make-tattoo-inks-out-ashes.html?utm_source=dgmodule&utm_medium=2&campaign=momme1 (accessed November 23, 2013).

Kasdorf, Julia Spicher. "To Pasture: 'Amish Forgiveness,' Silence, and the West Nickel Mines School Shooting." Cross Currents 59, no. 3 (2007): 328–347.

Keepers, Brie. E-mail interview by Candi Cann. A-1 Banner & Sign Company, April 3, 2013.

Kepner, Tyler. "For Yanks and Hokies, a Day of Remembrance." New York Times, March 19, 2008.

Kong, Lily. "No Place, New Places: Death and Its Rituals in Urban Asia." Urban Studies 49, no. 2 (2012): 415–433.

Kosut, Mary. "An Ironic Fad: The Commodification and Consumption of Tattoos." Journal of Popular Culture 39, no. 6 (2006): 1035–1048.

Kraybill, Donald. "Amish Memorials: The Nickel Mines Pasture and Quiet Forgiveness." Huffington Post, September 30, 2011. www

.huffingtonpost.com/donald-kraybill/amish-memorials-the-nickel-mines-memorial_b_982144.html (accessed March 18, 2013).

Krutak, Lars. "Scarification and Tattooing in Benin: The Bétamarribé Tribe of the Atakora Mountains." 2008. http://larskrutak.com/scarification-and-tattooing-in-benin-the-betamarribe-tribe-of-the-atakora-mountains/ (accessed May 11, 2012).

Laderman, Gary. *Rest in Peace: A Cultural History of Death and the Funeral Home in Twentieth-Century America*. New York: Oxford University Press, 2003.

LaFleur, William R. *Liquid Life: Abortion and Buddhism in Japan*. Princeton: Princeton University Press, 1994.

Laqueur, Thomas. "Cemeteries, Religion, and the Culture of Capitalism." In *Revival and Religion since 1700*, edited by Jane Garnett and Colin Matthew. London: Hambledon Press, 1993.

Laumann, A. E., and A. J. Derick. "Tattoos and Body Piercings in the United States: A National Data Set." *Journal of the American Academy of Dermatology* 55, no. 3 (2006): 413–421.

Lee, Kurtis. "Makeshift Memorial to Aurora Theater Shooting Victims Removed." *Denver Post*, September 20, 2012. www.denverpost.com/breakingnews/ci_21591061/aurora-removes-memorial-at-theater-shooting-site (accessed March 11, 2013).

Levine, Daniel H. "The Future of Christianity in Latin America." *Journal of Latin American Studies* 41, no. 1 (2009): 121–145.

Li-juan, Y. A. O. "Research on the Tattoo on the Women of Li People in Hainan Province." *Journal of the Central University for Nationalities* 3 (2005): 019.

Lindemann, Erich. "Symptomatology and Management of Acute Grief." *American Journal of Psychiatry* 101, no. 2 (1944): 141–148.

Lisa. Interview by Candi Cann. Audio recording. Koi Tattoo, Kailua, Hawaii, June 13, 2012.

Liu Lu. "Virtual Memorial." *China Daily*, April 11, 2011. http://usa.chinadaily.com.cn/life/2011–04/01/content_12262543.htm (accessed March 15, 2012).

Lloyd, Terrie. "Terrie's Job Tips: Death and Birth." *Daijob*. www.daijob.com/en/columns/terrie/article/334 (accessed November 29, 2013).

Maddrell, Avril, and James D. Sidaway, eds. *Deathscapes: Spaces for Death, Dying, Mourning and Remembrance*. Burlington, Vt.: Ashgate, 2010.

Marsden, William. "In Newtown, White Crosses, Tidy Lawns and Teddy Bears for Sale." *Windsor (Ont.) Star*, December 16, 2012. http://o.canada.com/2012/12/16/in-newtown-white-crosses-tidy-lawns-and-teddy-bears-for-sale/ (accessed March 21, 2013).

Matas, Kimberley. "Memorialize the Loss of Loved Ones." *Arizona Republic*, September 9, 2008. www.azcentral.com/arizonarepublic/local/articles/2008/09/09/20080909memorialtattoo0909.html (accessed July 5, 2012).

———. "Memorial Tattoos Ease Loss for Family, Friends." *Arizona Daily Star,* August 31, 2008. http://azstarnet.com/news/local/memorial-tattoos-ease-loss-for-family-friends/article_acafd753-a0c9-5c1d-867a-355b34db17a9.html (accessed April 19, 2013).

May, Michael. "The Skins They Carried: Military Tattoos in the Age of Iraq." *Texas Observer,* March 21, 2008. http://www.texasobserver.org/2722-the-skins-they-carried-military-tattoos-in-the-age-of-iraq/ (accessed May 21, 2012).

McCurry, Justin. "Mayor of Osaka Launches Crusade against Tattoos." *Guardian,* May 17, 2012. http://www.theguardian.com/world/2012/may/17/mayor-osaka-tattoos (accessed January 1, 2014).

McMullen, Ken. *Ghost Dance.* 1983 film. London: Mediabox Limited, 2008.

"Memorial Page for the Victims at Sandy Hook Elementary." https://www.facebook.com/121412NEWTOWNCT.

"Memorial Tattoo Question—Aw Sorry . . ." The Bump, Community Forum. http://forums.thebump.com/discussion/12164411/memorial-tattoo-question-aw-sorry (accessed January 1, 2014)

"Memorial Tattoos." www.facebook.com/media/set/?set=a.200381279984035.42812.200329196655910 (accessed May 21, 2012).

Merleau-Ponty, Maurice. *Phenomenology of Perception.* Translated by Colin Smith. London: Routledge, 1962.

Mona T-shirt. http://www.monatshirt.com/.

Morgan, John D., and Pittu Laungani, eds. *Death and Bereavement around the World.* 5 vols. Amityville, N.Y.: Baywood, 2002–2005.

Morin, Chrissy. "Aurora Shooting Memorial Service Time and Location." Examiner.com, July 22, 2012. www.examiner.com/article/aurora-shooting-memorial-service-and-community-gathering-for-victims (accessed April 4, 2013).

Morse, Dan. "Fraught Couture: Shirts for the Dead Are the New Rage in Some Inner Cities. They Memorialize Victims of Violence: Do They Glorify the Thug Life? 'More T-Shirts Than Friends.'" *Wall Street Journal,* February 4, 1999, A1.

Moser, Kate. "New Memorials: T-Shirts, Websites, Auto Decals." *Christian Science Monitor,* May 25, 2006, 15.

Mosle, Sara. "The Lives Unlived in Newtown." *New York Times Magazine,* December 30, 2012, 7.

Navarro, Marysa. "The Personal Is Political: Las Madres de Plaza de Mayo." In *Power and Popular Protest: Latin American Social Movements,* edited by Susan Eckstein. Berkeley: University of California Press, 1989, 241–258.

Neimeyer, Robert A., Darcy Harris, Howard Winokuer, and Gordon Thornton. *Grief and Bereavement in Contemporary Society: Bridging Research and Practice.* New York: Routledge, 2011.

Newhagen, J. E., and M. Ancell. "The Expression of Emotion and Social Status in the Language of Bumper Stickers." *Journal of Language and Social Psychology* 14, no. 3 (1995): 312–323.

"No Public Memorials Scheduled for Amish School Shootings." *National Catholic Reporter,* September 28, 2007, 3.

Obama, Barack. "Remarks on the Shootings in Newtown, Connecticut." *Daily Compilation of Presidential Documents,* December 14, 2012.

Office of Personnel Management, U.S. Government. "Fact Sheet: Definitions Related to Family Member and Immediate Relative for Purposes of Sick Leave, Funeral Leave, Voluntary Leave Transfer, Voluntary Leave Bank, and Emergency Leave Transfer." www.opm.gov/policy-data-oversight/pay-leave/leave-administration/fact-sheets/definitions-related-to-family-member-and-immediate-relative-for-purposes-of-sick-leave/ (accessed November 19, 2013).

Olyan, Saul M. *Biblical Mourning: Ritual and Social Dimensions.* New York: Oxford University Press, 2004.

Orsi, Robert A. *Between Heaven and Earth: The Religious Worlds People Make and the Scholars Who Study Them.* Princeton: Princeton University Press, 2005.

Owens, M. "Louisiana Roadside Memorials: Negotiating an Emerging Tradition." In *Spontaneous Shrines and the Public Memorialization of Death,* edited by Jack Santino. New York: Macmillan, 2006, 119–145.

Pew Research Center. "Millennials' Judgments about Recent Trends Not So Different." January 7, 2010. http://pewresearch.org/pubs/1455/millennial-generation-technological-communication-advances-societal-change (accessed July 7, 2012).

Plum, F. "Clinical Standards and Technological Confirmatory Tests in Diagnosing Brain Death." In *The Definition of Death: Contemporary Controversies,* edited by S. J. Younger, R. M. Arnold, and R. Schapiro. Baltimore: Johns Hopkins University Press, 1999, 34–65.

Poster, Mark. *The Mode of Information: Poststructuralism and Social Context.* Chicago: University of Chicago Press, 1990.

Powell, Robert Andrew. "Fitting Tribute." *Mother Jones,* May–June 2007, 58–63.

Quiring Monuments. www.monuments.com/living-headstones (accessed November 26, 2013).

"Recordatorios: Laura Raimon." *La Nacion.* April 25, 2013. http://servicios.lanacion.com.ar/edicion-impresa/avisos-funebres/resultado/categorias=1037,1039-fecha=20130425-pagina=1-palabra= (accessed April 26, 2013).

Rees, Dewi. *Death and Bereavement: The Psychological, Religious and Cultural Interfaces.* 2nd ed. London: Whurr, 2001.

Regalado, Francis. "Heinz Duerkop Filled Our Neighborhood with Happiness." *Borderzine,* January 7, 2011.

"Remembering Whitney." www.facebook.com/WhitneyHouston (accessed November 29, 2013).

"R.I.P. Juan Carlos (calaberilla) Raya." www.facebook.com/pages/RIP-Juan-Carlos-calaberilla-Raya/216657528383451 (accessed January 1, 2014).

"R.I.P. Sandy Hook Elementary School Children." www.facebook.com/RIPSandyHookElementaryChildren (accessed January 1, 2014).

"RIP Sandy Hook Elementary Victims." www.facebook.com/SandyRIPHook?fref=ts (accessed November 29, 2013).

Rivera, Ray. "Asking What to Do with Symbols of Grief as Memorials Pile Up." *New York Times,* January 5, 2013. www.nytimes.com/2013/01/06/nyregion/as-memorials-pile-up-newtown-struggles-to-move-on.html?pagewanted=1&_r=0 (accessed March 20, 2013).

Roberts, Pamela, and Lourdes A. Vidal. "Perpetual Care in Cyberspace: A Portrait of Memorials on the Web." *Omega: A Journal of Death and Dying* 40, no. 4 (2000): 521–546.

"Ruling of Tattoos in Islam." www.muslimconverts.com/cosmetics/tattoos.htm (accessed May 15, 2012).

Ryzik, Melena. "Spare Times: Around Town." *New York Times,* May 4, 2007.

"Sahih Bukhari Volume 003, Book 034, Hadith Number 440." *Haddith Collection.* www.hadithcollection.com/sahihbukhari/67-Sahih%20Bukhari%20Book%2034.%20Sales%20and%20Trade/2513-sahih-bukhari-volume-003-book-034-hadith-number-440.html (accessed May 5, 2013).

Sandell, Clayton. "Aurora Shooting Victims' Families Outraged by Invitation to Reopening." *ABC News,* January 2, 2013. http://abcnews.go.com/blogs/headlines/2013/01/aurora-shooting-victims-families-outraged-by-invitation-to-reopening/ (accessed March 12, 2013).

"Sandy Hook Elementary Remembered." www.facebook.com/SandyHook.Memorial.Site?ref=ts&fref=ts

"Sandy Hook Elementary School." www.facebook.com/SandyHook12.14.12?fref=ts (accessed November 29, 2013).

"Sandy Hook Elementary School Massacre Memorial Page." www.facebook.com/pages/Sandy-Hook-Elementary-School-Massacre-Memorial-Page/142591449223701?fref=ts (accessed November 29, 2013).

"Sandy Hook Promise." www.facebook.com/SandyHookPromise?fref=ts (accessed November 29, 2013)

Santino, Jack, ed. *Spontaneous Shrines and the Public Memorialization of Death.* New York: Palgrave Macmillan, 2006.

Saslow, Rachel. "Green Burials Return Dead to the Earth." *Washington Post,* June 12, 2011.

Scheinfeld, Noah. "Tattoos and Religion." *Clinics in Dermatology* 25, no. 4 (2007): 362–366.

Schmidt, Steve. "Car Culture Sees Decals as Mobile Memorials." *UT San Diego,* May 3, 2010. www.utsandiego.com/news/2010/may/03/car-culture-sees-decals-as-mobile-memorials/?print&page=all (accessed February 22, 2013).

Senie, H. F. "Mourning in Protest: Spontaneous Memorial and the Sacralization of Public Space." In *Spontaneous Shrines and the Public Memorialization of Death,* edited by Jack Santino. New York: Palgrave Macmillan, 2006, 41–56.

Shana. E-mail interview by Candi Cann. Mona T-Shirts, December 11, 2013.

Shane. Interview by Candi Cann. Audio recording. Eastside Tattoo, Kailua, Hawaii, June 14, 2012.

Shortell, Timothy. "Radicalization of Religious Discourse in El Salvador: The Case of Oscar A. Romero." *Sociology of Religion* 62, no. 1 (2001): 87–103.

"A Short History of the T-Shirt." *CBS News,* July 9, 2006. www.cbsnews. com/video/watch/?id=1786690n (accessed February 18, 2013).

Shreve, Jenn. "A Fitting Memorial: The Growing Popularity of the Memorial T-Shirt." *Slate.com,* August 26, 2003. www.slate.com/articles/news_and_politics/the_gist/2003/08/a_fitting_memorial.html (accessed January 12, 2013).

Smart, Carol. *Personal Life.* Cambridge, U.K.: Polity, 2007.

Stern, Barbara B., and Michael R. Solomon. "'Have You Kissed Your Professor Today?': Bumper Stickers and Consumer Self-Statements." *Advances in Consumer Research* 19, no. 1 (1992): 169–173. http://www.acrwebsite.org/search/view-conference-proceedings.aspx?Id=7289 (accessed January 1, 2014).

Stolberg, Sheryl Gay, and Robert Pear. "Wary Centrists Posing Challenge in Health Care Vote." *New York Times,* February 27, 2010. www.nytimes .com/2010/02/28/us/politics/28health.html (accessed February 28, 2010).

Stone, Elizabeth. "Grief in the Age of Facebook." *Chronicle of Higher Education,* February 28, 2010, B20.

Stucky, Nathalie-Kyoko, and Jake Adelstein. "In Japan, Tattoos Are Not Just for Yakuza Anymore." *Japan Sub-Culture,* January 2, 2013. www .japansubculture.com/in-japan-tattoos-are-not-just-for-yakuza-anymore/ (accessed May 5, 2013).

Szlemko, William J., et al. "Territorial Markings as a Predictor of Driver Aggression and Road Rage." *Journal of Applied Social Psychology* 38, no. 6 (2008): 1664–1688.

Tanner, Laura E. *Lost Bodies: Inhabiting the Borders of Life and Death.* Ithaca: Cornell University Press, 2006.

"Tattoo in Memory of Your Baby?" Netmums, http://www.netmums. com/coffeehouse/advice-support-40/miscarriage-stillbirth-loss-child-boards-548/miscarriage-stillbirth-loss-child-49/544555-tattoo-memory-your-baby-all.html (accessed January 7, 2014).

"Tattoo Update." The Bump, Community Forum. http://forums.thebump .com/discussion/12053978/tattoo-update-pip (accessed January 1, 2014).

Topa Cantisano, Gabriela, et al. "Apoyo Social Online e Identificación con el Grupo: Su Influencia Sobre las Quejas de Salud y la Satisfacción Vital." *Accion Psicológica* 7, no. 1 (2010): 53–64.

Torres-Salinas, Daniel. "Mark Zuckerberg, Fundador de Facebook, en la Universidad de Navarra." *Profesional de la Información* 17, no. 6 (2008): 681–684.

Trumpener, Katie. "Memories Carved in Granite: Great War Memorials and Everyday Life." *PMLA* 115 (2000): 1096–1103.

Tunsarawuth, Sinfah, and Todd Pittman. "Thailand Seeks to Ban Buddha Tattoos for Tourists." *Huffington Post,* June 2, 2011. www .huffingtonpost.com/2011/06/02/thailand-buddha-tattoo-ban_n_870336.html (accessed May 15, 2012).

Turkle, Sherry. *Life on the Screen: Identity in the Age of the Internet.* New York: Simon & Schuster, 1995.

Turner, Victor. *From Ritual to Theatre: The Human Seriousness of Play.* New York: Performing Arts Journal Publications, 1982.

———. "Passages, Margins, and Poverty: Religious Symbols of Communitas." In *The Anthropology of Politics: A Reader in Ethnography, Theory, and Critique,* edited by Joan Vincent. Oxford: Blackwell, 2002, 96–101.

———. *The Ritual Process: Structure and Anti-Structure.* Chicago: Aldine, 1969.

Usher, JoNell A., and Ulric Neisser. "Childhood Amnesia and the Beginnings of Memory for Four Early Life Events." *Journal of Experimental Psychology: General* 122, no. 2 (1993): 155.

Vail, D. Angus. "Tattoos Are Like Potato Chips . . . You Can't Have Just One: The Process of Becoming and Being a Collector." *Deviant Behavior* 20, no. 3 (1999): 253–273.

Verdery, Katherine. *The Political Lives of Dead Bodies.* New York: Columbia University Press, 1999.

Vergeer, Maurice, and Ben Pelzer. "Consequences of Media and Internet Use for Offline and Online Network Capital and Well-Being: A Causal Model Approach." *Journal of Computer-Mediated Communication* 15, no. 1 (2009): 189–210.

Vora, R. "Inscribe His Name: Tattoos and India's Ramnaami Community." *World and I* 12 (1997): 200–207.

Wakeman, Frederic. "Revolutionary Rites: The Remains of Chiang Kai-shek and Mao Tse-tung." *Representations* 10 (Spring 1985): 146–193.

Wang Hongyi. "Funeral Packed for Young Couple." *China Daily,* August 8, 2011. www.chinadaily.com.cn/china/2011-08/05/content_13053836 .htm&title=Funeral%20packed%20for%20young%20couple%7C Society%7Cchinadaily.com.cn (accessed February 28, 2012).

Watson, James Lee, and Evelyn S. Rawski, eds. *Death Ritual in Late Imperial and Modern China.* Berkeley: University of California Press, 1988.

Watson, Leon. "Etch-a-Fish Craze Is Condemned." *London Sun,* August 14, 2009. www.thesun.co.uk/sol/homepage/news/2588264/Etch-a-fish-craze-is-condemned.html (accessed May 14, 2012).

Weber, Max. *The Protestant Ethic and the Spirit of Capitalism.* Translated by Talcott Parsons. 1930. Reprint, London: Routledge, 1992.

Winchel, R. M., and M. Stanley. "Self-Injurious Behavior: A Review of the Behavior and Biology of Self-Mutilation." *American Journal of Psychiatry* 148, no. 3 (1991): 306–317.

Weiss, R. S. "Loss and Recovery." In *Handbook of Bereavement: Theory, Research, and Intervention,* edited by Margaret S. Stroebe, Wolfgang Stroebe, and Robert O. Hansson. New York: Cambridge University Press, 1993, 271–284.

Westlake, Adam. "Osaka Public Employee Applicants Face Required Tattoo Inspections after Ban." *Japan Daily Press,* August 8, 2012. http://japandailypress.com/osaka-public-employee-applicants-face-required-tattoo-inspections-after-ban-088620/ (accessed December 28, 2013).

Williams, Amanda L., and Michael J. Merten. "Adolescents' Online Social Networking Following the Death of a Peer." *Journal of Adolescent Research* 24, no. 1 (2009): 67–90.

———. "A Review of Online Social Networking Profiles by Adolescents: Implications for Future Research and Intervention." *Adolescence* 43, no. 170 (2008): 253–274.

Wortham, Jenna. "As Facebook Users Die, Ghosts Reach Out." *New York Times,* July 17, 2010. www.nytimes.com/2010/07/18/technology/18death.html (accessed February 27, 2012).

Xu Lin. "Virtually Immortal." *China Daily,* December 14, 2011. www.chinadaily.com.cn/cndy/2011-12/14/content_14261197.htm (accessed February 28, 2012).

Yamada, Mieko. "Westernization and Cultural Resistance in Tattooing Practices in Contemporary Japan." *International Journal of Cultural Studies* 12, no. 4 (2009): 319–338.

Yardley, William. "Portland, Ore., Acts to Protect Cyclists." *New York Times,* January 10, 2008.

"Yolanda S. Cuevas, In Memoriam. " *Waco Tribune-Herald,* April 25, 2013. www.legacy.com/ns/obitfinder/obituary-search.aspx?daterange=2010-2013&firstname=yolanda&lastname=cuevas&countryid=1&stateid=57&affiliateid=all (accessed November 30, 2013).

Young, Craig, and Duncan Light. "Corpses, Dead Body Politics and Agency in Human Geography: Following the Corpse of Dr. Petru Groza." *Transactions of the Institute of British Geographers* 38, no. 1 (2013): 135–148.

Young, Kirsty. "Social Ties, Social Networks and the Facebook Experience." *International Journal of Emerging Technologies and Society* 9, no. 1 (2011): 30–34.

Index

Page numbers that appear in *italics* refer to illustrations.

MATERIAL WORLDS

Books in this series explore worlds of our own making. Emphasizing interdisciplinary perspectives on material culture, authors interpret the ways in which individuals and communities create environments, traditions, and symbols from art, architecture, furnishing, food, and dress. In addition to interpreting the cultural values that artifacts and environments reveal, the series sheds light on the diversity of material worlds across the social landscape. Whether remote or close to home, the worlds uncovered by this series reflect the ways that "material" and "culture" come together in everyday lives.

SERIES EDITOR
Simon J. Bronner

Virtual Afterlives: Grieving the Dead in the Twenty-First Century
Candi K. Cann

Designing the Centennial: A History of the 1876 International Exhibition in Philadelphia
Bruno Giberti

Culinary Tourism
edited by Lucy M. Long

Funeral Festivals in America: Rituals for the Living
Jacqueline S. Thursby